Welsh Three Thousand Challenges

A Guide For Walkers and Hill Runners

by Roy Clayton and Ronald Turnbull
with Foreword and History by Harvey Lloyd
maps and sketches by John Gillham

Grey Stone Books
Hoddlesden

Ronald Turnbull 1997
Roy Clayton 1993/1997
ISBN 0 9515996 6 6

British Library Cataloguing in Publication Data:
A catalogue record of this book is available from the British
Library

Also by Ronald Turnbull: Across Scotland on Foot (Grey Stone)
Forthcoming 1997: Long Days in Lakeland (Grey Stone)
Coast to Coast (Dalesman Trail Guide)

Acknowledgments:
We would like to thank those who have helped us in the publication of
this book; Harvey Lloyd, who has been a major source of detailed knowledge of the area; Colin Donnelly for photos and accounts of his Welsh
3000s record; James Clayton, Anthony Wilson, Kieran Hartley and Glyn
Jones for their company on the hills; Ken Vickers for his invaluable
advice; Ian Waddell for creating the unique Dragon's Back race as well as
information and photos of it; Depot Para, Aldershot (The Parachute
Regiment) for food and shelter on the Dragon's Back; John Cleare for his
inspiring photos of Joss Naylor; and John Gillham for his maps and
sketches, support and encouragement and also for his car support on the
Paddy Buckley Round. Unless stated otherwise photographs are by Roy
Clayton or John Gillham.

Cover Photo: Joss Naylor on Crib Goch during his record-
breaking Welsh Three Thousands run of 1973: by **John
Cleare/Mountain Camera Picture Library**

Printed by Carnmor, London Road, Preston

Contents

Foreword

My foreword could begin like a child's story. "Once upon a time there was a man named E.G. Rowland, who liked to walk amongst the Welsh Hills and decided to write a book called *Hill Walking in Snowdonia*"....

E.G. Rowland was one of the people who introduced me to the region nearly forty years ago – forty years that have brought to me the most wonderful experiences. Known even in the fifties as "the old man of the mountains", the written words of this veteran rambler and mountaineer became part of the motivation and inspiration leading to the upturn in interest in hill walking in the fifties.

Until recently I was a youth hostel warden at Pen y Pass and lived amongst these glorious mountains. I was delighted when approached by Roy Clayton to help with this book. In putting it together Roy, Ronald Turnbull and myself hope that it will spread the call of the mountains to a wider public.

My first attempt at the Welsh Three Thousands took place on a Sunday in June. At 5 am I am never at my best and peering into a cloudy environment crisscrossed with the beams of head-torches was not encouraging for a novice of long mountain treks. I was accompanied by a group of experienced mountain people, however, and I had worked at getting fit. It was a case of head down and hope for better weather later in the day. Luck was with us and we came through the cloud on Crib Goch - the cotton wool layer below extending towards Anglesey and the Irish Sea. The sun warmed our cold limbs. Suddenly Snowdon was a wonderful place to be.

The day progressed well. Support groups in Nant Peris and Ogwen supplied much needed sustenance. The traverse of the Carneddau was highlighted by a glorious setting sun, diluting the pain and fatigue that the day's rigours had brought about.

The next attempt was quite different. The day again started wet and miserable but the traverse of Crib Goch, Carnedd

Ugain and Snowdon passed reasonably well. The trouble started on the descent to Nant Peris. A bad choice of route and laziness in not consulting a compass, brought us to very steep ground above Cwm Glas Bach and delayed our arrival in the village until late morning. The weather continued to deteriorate and morale was low. The Glyders were very wet and the attempt was aborted at Ogwen. We learned from our foolishness. A compass in the rucksack does not help in route finding, even in the hills we thought we knew so well!

Finally a word about conservation of the environment over which we travel. The National Parks are managed to promote "quiet enjoyment" for the population. Headlines such as "Charity runners threaten Snowdon" in the newspapers suggest an increased resistance to any sort of organised event. The land in the Snowdonia National Park is largely privately owned and the route crosses several ecologically sensitive sites - Snowdonia is well known for its rare alpine plants. In addition to this local farmers are finding it increasingly difficult to make a living from rearing sheep on such hostile terrain. The problems have been made worse by the increasing numbers of walkers and it is important that everybody should be concerned to protect this fragile region. Always follow the Country Code and be considerate to landowners and other landusers.

The popularity of the Welsh 3's has been firmly established. The greats will continue to work at knocking minutes off existing records; the also-rans will try to better their previous times and the mountains will always be there for anyone, whether rich or poor – to walk over to run over or simply to admire from the comfort of valley or village.

Harvey Lloyd, Nantgwynant

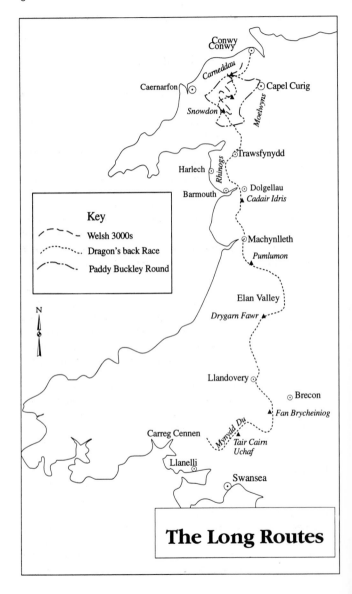

The Long Routes

Introduction

Snowdon, Tryfan, Crib Goch: names to stir the blood – and bootsoles – of any mountain man or woman. My first acquaintance with these peaks was on one of those whistle-stop coach tours. The driver proudly pointed out the peaks of Snowdon, the principality's highest mountain but my senses were more stirred by the rugged ramparts of the Glyder Range on the other side of the coach. Later in the day, standing on the shores of Llyn Ogwen, my eyes were drawn up to to the intimidating crest of Tryfan. I watched as climbers grappled with the hard rocky buttresses, while walkers with brightly coloured cagouls clambered towards the skyline. The seeds of my interest in the mountains were sewn.

A couple of years later, I ventured onto the hills as a member of a school-party intent on doing four days of the Pennine Way. Not even the cumbersome pack that was hoisted onto my back could subdue my high spirits as we set forth from Malham. Fifty miles later I sat on the return coach yearning for a hot bath, but content in the knowledge that I would never again have to set foot on another mountain. Why then did I say yes when the teacher, Jim Pickering, asked if I would be interested in further excursions? Was it that I actually enjoyed battling against driving rain and gale-force winds, soaked to the bone by damp impenetrable mists? Had I derived some perverse pleasure from the wet peat that slurped around my boots, inside and out?

Quite quickly I became the perfect peak-bagger. The lists at the back of my Wainwright and Poucher were sprinkled with little ticks. Eventually, I stood again at the foot of Tryfan, which was to be my first Welsh Three Thousander. All routes to the top are mercilessly steep and I forged up the north ridge with a sense of exhilaration and purpose. At the top I was rewarded with views as good as I have seen anywhere in the world. That day I covered as many miles as I possibly could, seeking out every delightful corner of Glyder Fach, Glyder Fawr and Y Garn before descending the mystical Devil's Kitchen. I was spellbound – like a child let loose in a chocolate factory.

Like many mountain men before me, I was fascinated by Thomas Firbank's account of the Welsh Three Thousands race in his book *I Bought a Mountain*. It was Firbank who laid down the basic rules that stand today: i.e. that the race starts on the top of Snowdon, finishes on Foel Fras and that the tops of all the eligible summits must be touched on the way.

In those days it was accepted that there were fourteen summits with a drop of at least fifty feet in all directions. Since the Ordnance Survey's remeasurement, the Carneddau peak of Y Garnedd Uchaf has been judged to be 3038 feet above sea level and thus has been added to the list. If you adhered to the Scottish 'Munro' rules there would only be eight Welsh Three Thousands. Crib Goch, Carnedd Ugain, Glyder Fach, Pen yr Ole Wen, Yr Elen, Foel Grach and Carnedd Uchaf would all be omitted. Conversely I have heard it said that Castell y Gwynt on Glyder Fach and Clogwyn y Person on Carnedd Ugain would qualify under the fifty foot rule. Mathematics has no business in the mountains and I do not wish to get bogged down in classification of what constitutes a peak or mountain. Nobody will make me believe Crib Goch is not a true mountain.

The Three Thousands route is 27 miles long from the top of Snowdon to Rowen youth hostel. It involves some 13,000ft of ascent – a very serious expedition, especially in less than perfect conditions, for it crosses some of the most rugged mountains in British Isles. The inexperienced may well be intimidated by the exposed ridges and steep descents.

The terrain is diverse. Snowdon's is one of magnificent rock slabs and pyramids linked by razor-edge ridges. The Glyders are every bit as rugged – a chaos of bouldery summits and craggy, lake-filled cwms. The Carneddau's wide, grassy plateaux are a delight to walk but can be confusing when the mist hangs low. Never is the need for a compass so great as on the Carneddau.

Some may feel that the twenty-seven miles is a task too great to be completed in one day and may wish to divide the walk into more manageable sections. Enjoyable ways to accomplish these are by youth hostelling or backpacking. The Youth

Hostel Association has made many improvements over the years. They can now offer comfortable accommodation and a chance to socialise with people with similar interests. The hostels are listed in the data section at the back of the book. Backpacking offers a great flexibility of schedule – you can stop and pitch when you have had enough for there are many wonderful high-level wild campsites on all three mountain ranges in addition to the conveniently placed official valley sites. It must be stressed however that the route is only suitable for experienced backpackers. Steep descents and loose screes are more dangerous with the encumbrance of a heavy rucksack.

I felt that it would be a good idea to include sections on the Snowdon Horseshoe and also the Welsh One Thousand Metres Race, now known as the Snowdonia Summits Marathon. Both are classic routes in their own right and offer a different perspective on the mountains of the region.

Ronald Turnbull gets up his hills somewhat faster than I do. He's not content with just fifteen peaks, but will show you how to do the forty-seven of them in the Paddy Buckley Round and even more in the Dragon's Back, a race devised by Ian Waddell and loosely based on the Snowdonia to Gower route.

It has been fifteen years since that first memorable journey over the Pennines and, in that time, I have never lost my feeling for mountain country. I am still spellbound by Wales; I am still drawn to its mountains. I have tramped the same ground many times, but no two walks have ever been the same; the sun's rays, shadows cast by clouds, secretive mists and gleaming snows have each interpreted in their own way the timeless mountainscapes.

Roy Clayton: Blackpool December 1996

In the dark days of 1940 wartime Britain found its imagination captured by the account of an Englishman turned Welsh sheep farmer. Embedded in the agricultural matter of *I Bought a Mountain*, like grit in an old sock, is the achievement of a record about which very few had even heard: the fourteen three thousand foot peaks of Wales, in a time of under nine hours. In the late sixties I was just learning what 3000ft of ascent actually means in terms of exhaustion, peppermint sweeties and total separation from the world below. I read with fascinated incomprehension the exploits of Joss Naylor. He covered nearly eleven thousand feet over fifteen Welsh mountains in four and three quarter hours: that's how long it took the teenage me to climb just one Munro.

Twenty years later, I discovered for myself the pains and pleasures of fell running. Incomprehension shrank, while so did the times: mine across the hills of Scotland and those across the Welsh Threes, with Colin Donnelly recording a mere 4 hrs 20 mins in 1988.

For the ordinary but ambitious hillwalker the Welsh 3000s route is a once-in-a-lifetime 24-hour challenge. Among such ultimate walks (the Lakes 3000s, the Lyke Wake Walk, the Yorkshire Three Peaks) we think that the Welsh 3000s is the finest. The ordinary fellrunner, in pursuit of his own eccentric excellence, submits to hours of training under winter streetlights, years of twisted ankles, knee-damage and even a horrible mauve and orange club vest. The reward for all this is that the likes of the Welsh 3000s becomes a simple day trip; a substantial day trip, certainly, but still one of perhaps a half dozen

Colin Donnelly on Foel Fras after breaking the Welsh 3000s record in 1988.

such outings in the Summer. Well, until that knee injury comes back.

Such runners may be aiming for a fast time, whether that's Thomas Firbank's 8½ hours, or 6 hours, or even Colin Donnelly's 4 hours 20 minutes. These will take a conventional 'downhill' direction, and study carefully Route Variation S2, which saves nearly two minutes on the descent from Crib Goch. Others may run it purely for pleasure. They may take it southbound, knowing their extra speed will let them take in the scrambling ascents of Tryfan and of Glyder Fawr's Bristly Ridge, and still get to Snowdon in time for the last train down.

For runners, the once-in-a-lifetime 24-hour challenge is the round of 47 tops devised by Paddy Buckley.

Starting from Llanberis, Buckley's Round traverses the Glyderau and the southern Carneddau before climbing Moel Siabod from Plas y Brenin. It continues over the Moelwyns to Cnicht, then crosses to the range west of Snowdon known as the Eifionydd. Finally, it makes a long high crossing of the Snowdon group to finish over Moel Eilio. It's an even better route than the well-known Bob Graham Round of the English Lake District, for at seven different points it runs along the high sharp ridges. These, whether of grass or rock, are the best of running or of walking.

The Paddy Buckley Round is also even longer than the Bob Graham Round. At 62 miles, with 29,000ft of ascent and no relaxing road sections, it turns out to be that annoying little bit more than ordinary runners can manage in the time. But, as it's such fun, why not linger over it? Pack up a little lightweight tent and take it over two days (which is still pretty vigorous), over four days (which is hard walking) or a week (for those who take their lingering seriously). At whatever speed, it's an intensive experience of high Snowdonia and a truly over-the-top backpack expedition.

Over even more tops was the Dragon's Back of 1992. For a taste of the full splendour and absurdity of fell running I add a brief account of this, the longest ever run over the British hills. Over five days, two hundred miles and 45,000 ft of ascent, it stretched the concept of going up Snowdon to the limit and well beyond.

Ronald Turnbull, Thornhill December 1996

Descending to Ogwen with Pen yr Ole Wen towering to the skies.
Photo: Roy Clayton

The Welsh Three Thousands

by Roy Clayton

History & Records
by Harvey Lloyd

Who it was that first donned his boots and set off for the summit of Yr Wyddfa with the intentions of traversing the Welsh three thousand foot peaks in one go is lost in the history of mountaineering. It would probably be in Victorian times,perhaps from a small hotel such as the Pen y Gwryd or Pen y Pass. It is recorded that Eustace Thomas of the Manchester-based Rucksack Club walked it in 1919 with a group of friends. His time, twenty-two and a half hours, seems unremarkable enough but, considering he had passed his fiftieth birthday and had not taken up long distance walking until the previous year, it becomes more creditable. He had been described as an ageing business man with a weak digestion, troublesome feet and the beginnings of an elderly spread.

The walker of this time had none of today's high tech gear. Heavy boots, tweeds, poor waterproofs and little equipment was balanced, however, by a great enthusiasm for the hills and the challenge they issued. These men were true pioneers!

In the early days the route followed was nearly as variable as the times taken. Parties started from Nantgwynant, Llanberis, Pen-y-Gwryd and Aber. The idea of starting and finishing at the same place to make a round trip with no transport problems was soon adopted, the Llanberis or Ogwen Valleys being the main starting/finishing points. The *Locked Book* at the Pen y Gwryd Hotel is a mine of information on these early attempts. Many visitors to this hotel took on board the traverse of the Welsh 3's. They realised that there was a record to be broken in addition to

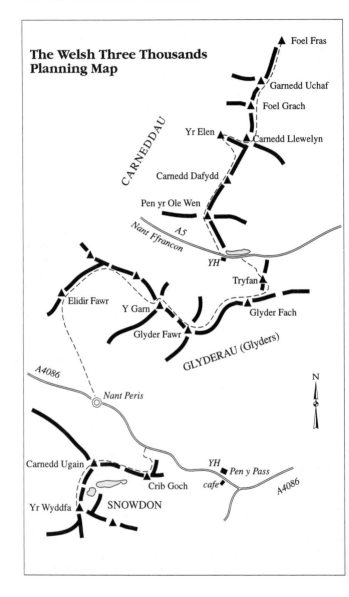

The Welsh Three Thousands Planning Map

Foel Fras

Garnedd Uchaf

Foel Grach

Yr Elen

Carnedd Llewelyn

CARNEDDAU

Carnedd Dafydd

Pen yr Ole Wen

Nant Ffrancon

A5

YH

Tryfan

Elidir Fawr

Y Garn

Glyder Fach

Glyder Fawr

GLYDERAU (Glyders)

A4086

Nant Peris

N

Carnedd Ugain

YH Pen y Pass

Crib Goch

cafe

A4086

Yr Wyddfa

SNOWDON

the pleasure of a long day on the hills. Philips and Clay managed to fit in a hearty breakfast at the PYG and a forty minute tea-stop at Ogwen Cottage in a trip that took seventeen hours.

Herbert Carr, in *The Mountains of Snowdonia*, published in 1925, must have been instrumental in encouraging many of the early attempts. He wrote:

"Strong walkers will not visit Snowdonia many times without wishing to include the Carnedds, the Glyders and Snowdon in a single expedition. It is a very fine walk and, under favourable conditions, very well worth doing. In length it is about thirty miles when taken from Beddgelert, Conwy or Llanfairfechan. From thirteen to fourteen hours may be allowed, halts included, at an ordinary pace. It can be reduced by making the Ogwen Valley and Pen y Pass the points of departure and arrival. If part of the walk has to be done in the dark it is best to reserve the paths of Snowdon for the night watches. A moon, preferably full, is to be desired."

Carr does not tell us if he attempted the walk himself but he was obviously writing to the 'hard men' of the twenties. By the thirties the writer Showell Stiles had finished the route in twelve hours forty-four minutes and then Frank Shuttleworth achieved ten hours twenty-nine minutes.

Thomas Firbank set the scene for the post Second World War upsurge in interest. A fascinating account of his own record attempt is given in his book *I Bought a Mountain*. He colourfully described the rigorous training he and his wife, Esme adopted for the event. They looked for ways to modify the route and came up with the idea of descending Crib Goch's north ridge, thus saving valuable miles. In the Spring of 1938, the well publicised record attempt took place and the roadsides of Nant Peris were lined with spectators. On the summit of Snowdon the newspapermen were gathered in anticipation of a new record. The competitors were regally conveyed to the summit by a specially laid on train. Thomas Firbank did set the record along with companions W.E. Capel Cure and R.M. Hamer, reaching Foel Fras in a time of eight hours and twenty-five minutes. Esme, accompanied by Thomas Davies and hampered

Joss Naylor descends the scree slopes on Crib Goch during his record-breaking crossing of the Welsh 3000s in 1973
Photo by John Cleare/Mountain Camera Picture Library

by a foot injury, limped home in an equally impressive time of nine hours twenty-nine minutes. Firbank prophesied that

SPLIT TIMES

COLIN DONNELLY'S RECORD RUN - 11th June 1988
Sponsored by Reebock
Start time 10.30 am.

Peak	Split Time	Time from Start
SNOWDON		
Yr Wyddfa		
Carnedd Ugain	4.56 mins	4.56mins
Crib Goch	9.33	14.27
Blaen Nan	14.54	29.23
Nant Peris PO	7.32	36.50
THE GLYDERS		
Elidir Fawr	36.10	1hr13.00
Y Garn	22.00	1 35.00
Glyder Fawr	19.00	1 54.00
Glyder Fach	9.18	2 03.18
Tryfan	16.42	2 20.00
Ogwen	13.00	2 33.00
THE CARNEDDAU		
Pen yr Ole Wen	38.00	3 11.00
Carnedd Dafydd	11.00	3 22.00
Yr Elen	20.00	3 42.00
Carnedd Llewelyn	12.00	3 54.00
Foel Grach	10.40	4 04.40
Carnedd Uchaf	6.04	4 10.44
Foel Fras	9.12	4 19.56

Pacers - Don Williams, Emlyn Roberts, Del Davies, Huw Parry
and Fon Williams

ANGELA CARSON'S RECORD RUN - 5th August 1989

Angela Carson, running for the Eryri Harriers, broke the womens' record. Sponsored by Reebock.
Start time 10.30 am.

Peak	Split Time	Time from Start
SNOWDON		
Yr Wyddfa		
Carnedd Ugain	5.25 mins	5.25 mins
Crib Goch	13.38	19.03
Nant Peris	35.13	54.16
THE GLYDERS		
Elidir Fawr	41.20	1hr35.36
Y Garn	26.58	2 02.34
Glyder Fawr	23.11	2 25.45
Glyder Fach	10.26	2 36.11
Tryfa	24.19	3 00.30
Ogwen	23.42	3 24.12
THE CARNEDDAU		
Pen yr Ole Wen	38.50	4 03.02
Carnedd Dafydd	20.20	4 23.22
Yr Elen	23.55	4 47.17
Carnedd Llewelyn	13.03	5 00.20
Foel Grach	12.48	5 13.08
Carnedd Uchaf	6.23	5 19.31
Foel Fras	9.10	5 28.41

Pacers Trefor Jones, Alan T Williams, David Carson and Tony Barker

one day somebody would complete the journey in seven and a half hours but not much faster! Firbank's successful attempt brought to the forefront the simmering controversy that had been around for sometime, "Should the mountaineer run in the mountains?" The attempt was frowned upon by the establishment and resulted in an apology by Firbank's companions being published in the Climbers' Club Journal for 1939. There was no doubt that it was not the done thing for members of the club to take part in such escapades that produce "some rather unwelcome publicity in the press".

The fifties brought the athletes to the hills. John Disley set seven hours twenty-four minutes and Chris Brasher and friends clocked six hours dead. The sixties saw Eric Beard home in the "impossible" time of five hours thirteen minutes. Just before his untimely death in a car crash in 1969 "Beardie" had been on a training run with a friend, Joss Naylor whom he predicted would take his records. On a damp, misty June morning in 1973 this shepherd from Wasdale took up that offer and set off from the summit of Snowdon. It was only the fourth time he had been to Wales, and he became cragfast on the damp rocks of Crib Goch. "Thirty-five minutes to the road", he records with a hint of dissatisfaction. Unfamiliarity led him to a poor route up Glyder Fach's summit boulderpile. On Carnedd Llewelyn he lost more time and only the appearance of three Welshmen out of the mist saved him from going seriously astray. But four hours forty-six minutes later, still in mist, he touched the summit of Foel Fras. Joss's verdict: there's about ten minutes to come off that time.

The record was to stand until 1988 when Colin Donnelly, a member of the Eryri Harriers, recorded an unbelievable four hours nineteen minutes, including Carnedd Uchaf, a new summit added to the earlier list of fourteen by the latest Ordnance Survey maps. Colin was accompanied and paced by his team-mates from the Harriers. Donnelly, like Naylor, wasn't entirely happy with his run. "Shouldn't have been so tired on the Carneddau, really should have knocked a further ten minutes off." Perhaps someone reading this book will prove Donnelly wrong with his ten minutes – as Joss Naylor, John Barford, Thomas Firbank have all been wrong before him – and take the Welsh Three

Walkers at Bwlch Goch with Crib Goch towering behind

Thousands record below four hours.

The females too have left their mark with some very creditable times. Angela Carson ran five hours twenty-eight minutes in 1989 to put herself in the record books.

An event of this nature holds glory for all that take part. The group of schoolboys that accomplished a complete round of the 3000's from Pen-y-gwryd with Dr. G. Linsey Jones in sixteen hours two minutes must have been very pleased with themselves, and one wonders how John Wagstaff felt in 1978 after completing the route three times in twenty-two hours forty-nine minutes.

THE SNOWDON GROUP

The Summits

Yr Wyddfa	**3560ft (1085 m)**
Carnedd Ugain*	**3493ft (1065)**
Crib Goch	**3026ft (924)**

* incorrectly named Garnedd Ugain on current O.S. Maps

Wales' mountains are firmly routed in its culture and heritage and none is greater than Snowdon, the Principality's highest summit and also the highest south of the Scottish Border. The Snowdon Group consists of five major peaks - Y Lliwedd, Yr Aran, Carnedd Ugain (sometimes referred to as Crib y Ddysgl), Crib Goch and Yr Wyddfa (the more acceptable Welsh name for Snowdon itself).

Yr Wyddfa, which means the tomb, has, in terms of mountain architecture, few peers within the United Kingdom. Its pointed summit is guarded by precipitous cliffs and, not surprisingly, affords the most spectacular panoramas in all Wales. They include the wide sweep of Cardigan Bay and the northern coastline. A dozen or so lakes and tarns of various sizes glint in the valleys and cwms. Dominant among them is Llyn Llydaw, which fills the huge Cwm Dyli. Many people feel Snowdon has been spoilt by the construction of the railway and summit hotel (cafe). John Gillham wrote in his book 'Snowdonia to the Gower', "The flat-roofed monstrosity of Snowdon's 'hotel' and railway terminus is hated by all when closed but used by most when open." I certainly despised it when arriving hot and bothered ten minutes after closing time.

The two foot seven inch gauge rack railway was opened in 1896 and had a tragic accident on the first day. On the descent a train was derailed and tumbled down the mountainside, narrowly missing several climbers. One person died - a passenger who leapt out of a moving carriage. The trains have since carried millions of joyful travellers to the

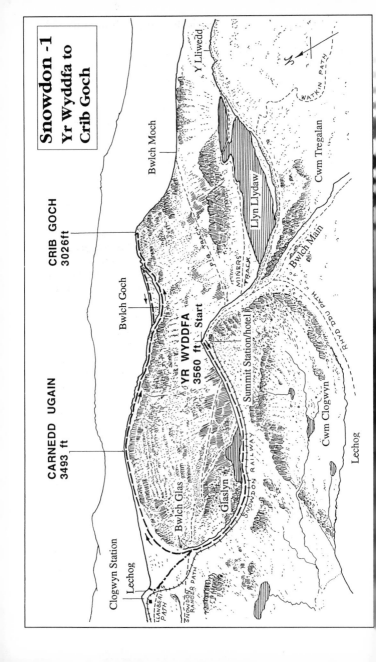

Snowdon -1
Yr Wyddfa to Crib Goch

CARNEDD UGAIN 3493 ft

CRIB GOCH 3026ft

Bwlch Moch

Y Lliwedd

Bwlch Goch

WATKIN PATH

Clogwyn Station

Lechog

Bwlch Glas

Glaslyn

YR WYDDFA 3560 ft Start

Llyn Llydaw

Summit Station/hotel

MINERS TRACK

PIG TRACK

Bwlch Main

Cwm Tregalan

LLANBERIS PATH

SNOWDON RANGER PATH

SNOWDON RAILWAY

Cwm Clogwyn

RHYD DDU PATH

Lechog

rooftop of Wales. To some, including myself, it is comforting to see the plumes of smoke from the little steam engines billowing from the high ridges, or the sound of their hoots echoing through the mists.

Crib Goch and its Pinnacles are probably the most exhilarating part of the Three Thousands. I vividly remember my first visit. The cloud base was barely over fifteen hundred feet and wispy grey mist swirled around my feet as I trod gingerly over the damp rock of the crest. It was an eerie experience and I could only imagine the drop through the clouds to the valley below.

Snowdon is steeped in history and legend. Ghostly relics of the old copper mines and quarries litter many routes to the top. In legend, King Arthur fought with the treacherous Sir Mordred at Cwm Tregalan (south of the summit). In the bloody battle Arthur forced his foe into a retreat up the mountain to the pass between Yr Wyddfa and Y Lliwedd, but was hit by an arrow. Before dying, he slew Sir Modred with the mighty sword Excalibur. The place has been known since as Bwlch y Saethau (Pass of the Arrows).

Beneath Bwlch y Saethau lies Glaslyn. Romantics believe that in its bottomless depths lives a fearsome monster, Afanc. The beast once lived in Llyn-yr-Afanc, near Betws-y-Coed, where he would often create severe floods. One day, after a particularly bad wetting, Afanc's neighbours decided to act. They knew this beast had an eye for the ladies, and with the help of a beautiful damsel, lured him from the pool while they hid behind the bushes. As the amorous monster made an appearance the villagers set on him. After binding poor Afanc in chains they dragged him across mountains and valleys before dumping him in Glaslyn. Some say he lives there still. Other less romantic souls say he was just a beaver. Well, you know how these Welshmen exaggerate!

Snowdon – The Route
Yr Wyddfa (Snowdon) to Nant Peris
Distance 4 miles (6.5 km)

After taking a last look from Yr Wyddfa's summit (always

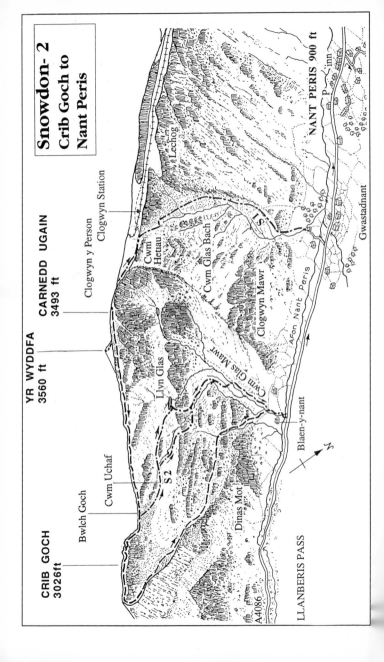

**Snowdon- 2
Crib Goch to
Nant Peris**

CRIB GOCH
3026ft

YR WYDDFA
3560 ft

CARNEDD UGAIN
3493 ft

Bwlch Goch

Cwm Uchaf

S2

Llyn Glas

Clogwyn y Person

Clogwyn Station

Cwm
Hetiau

'r Lechog

NANT PERIS 900 ft

P—inn

Gwastadnant

S1

Cwm Glas Bach

Cwm Glas Mawr

Clogwyn Mawr

Afon Nant Peris

Blaen-y-nant

Dinas Mot

A4086

LLANBERIS PASS

N

start at the trig point), the marathon begins. Descend in a NNW direction, keeping to the path close to the edge of the huge corrie of Cwm Dyli and parallel to the line of the mountain railway. Bwlch Glas, the pass between Yr Wyddfa itself and Carnedd Ugain, is soon reached. The spot is marked by a huge obelisk and is the place where walkers using both the Miners' and Pig Tracks gain the ridge. The obtrusive obelisk was erected by the National Park to provide a waymark when winter snows lie deep. Before its construction, the upper regions of the Pig Track were uncertain and obscure in such conditions.

Beyond the obelisk, a sprawling cairn marks the departure of the popular Llanberis track. The route veers slightly to the right, still keeping to the edge of Cwm Dyli. The wide, cairned track affords an easy pace as it climbs towards **Carnedd Ugain**, whose grassy top (3493 ft) is crowned by a trig point. Although the views to Llanberis and the Glyders are striking, the knife-edged ridge to the Pinnacles of Crib Goch captures most attention.

On descending Carnedd Ugain you are confronted by a choice of well-worn paths. This can be confusing in mist. It is advisable to maintain an easterly direction, close to the edge of Cwm Dyli, as this is where the path materialises when the ridge narrows. After dropping down into a hollow there is a magnificent view of Yr Wyddfa. The crest of the ridge is now followed before veering a few feet to the left of a rocky buttress. In favourable conditions the arete itself is the finest course as the climber is challenged to clamber over half a mile of rocky bluffs and clefts. The use of hands will be needed here. The course ceases to be obvious as the ridge appears to terminate abruptly at a cliff face. A path is available to the right however. It descends steeply some fifty feet by a series of ledges to a broad grassy pass, **Bwlch Goch** (marked Coch on current maps).

The lofty crests of the **Crib Goch Pinnacles**, which now lie ahead, form the most demanding obstacle of the route. The most satisfying way is the one over the knife-edged crest, although this is very exposed and not suitable for those with a nervous disposition. They should use the devious path circumventing the pinnacles on the Cwm

Dyli side (right). The higher route starts its ascent on the right hand side of the first pinnacle, where a steep path quickly attains the top and drops down the left side to the depression. The second pinnacle is tackled from the left side, to pass a pile of stones marking the true summit (3026ft). This is exciting stuff – Snowdonia is laid beneath your feet. Teasing glimpses of Cwm Uchaf and Llyn Glas add to the drama of the situation. The final stage to **Crib Goch's** northern and more celebrated summit (3023 ft) is the narrowest of all but, as with the Pinnacles, there is an easier route just below and to the right of the crest, which is used as a handrail. This second summit is marked by a circular rock platform and a meeting of ridges.

Some walkers will descend Crib Goch eastwards, by way of Bwlch Moch, to their journey's end at Pen y Pass, but the Welsh 3000's is barely started. Here the excitement continues on the arete, which curves northwards, encircling the rugged **Cwm Uchaf** and descending steeply towards the Pass of Llanberis*.

All that you have gained on Snowdon is lost on the descent. Care needs to be exercised on this exposed spur. After half a mile of rapid descent, a precipitous scree path descends westwards off the ridge, thus avoiding the vast cliffs of Dinas Mot. The scramble leads to a wet, grassy bowl, fringed by crags. Here the eastern banks of a stream (GR 622557), marked "falls" on the 1:25000 map, are followed *(water source)*. The track by the tumbling stream leads into **Cwm Glas Mawr** and beneath the huge rocky knoll of Dinas Mot.

After passing a sheepfold, a pleasant walk by stream-side pastures leads to the road at Blaen-y-nant. The twisting narrow road is then followed for one and a half miles to the little village of **Nant Peris**.

---

* See Variation S1, which requires steps to be retraced along the Pinnacles to Bwlch Moch - for fast running times only.

THE GLYDERAU (GLYDERS)

The Summits

Glyder Fawr	3279ft	(996m)
Glyder Fach	3262ft	(990)
Y Garn	3104ft	(947)
Elidir Fawr*	3029ft	(923)
Tryfan	3010ft	(915)

* The more correct name for this mountain is Carnedd Elidir.

From Capel Curig westwards stretches a ten mile range of hard granite that has long been my favourite tramping ground. The Glyderau or Glyders as they are often (but incorrectly) called, include some of Wales' most rugged peaks and issue a stern challenge for the hardiest walker. Five of our 3000 footers are located here. The Glyderau's northern faces above Ogwen are bold, with deeply gouged cwms and magnificent sculpted cliffs and crags. Several of the cwms contain delightful tarns.

Highest of the range, although only by a few feet, is Glyder Fawr, a rugged mountain with a large summit plateau of splintered rock and several jagged outcrops. The overall terrain is not unlike one would imagine the surface of the moon to be. Glyder Fawr's next door neighbour, Glyder Fach, has even more spectacular features. Castell y Gwynt (Castle of the Winds) is a gaunt and massive serrated outcrop soaring from a sea of boulders. It forms a formidable obstruction to walkers from Glyder Fawr (most walk around its base). The Cantilever slab, set slightly back from the summit, is a huge slab of rock that seems precariously perched on an offset fulcrum. In fact it has been there for thousands of years and has withstood the weight of the many travellers posing for their "all conquering" summit snapshots. Glyder Fach's most powerful feature has to be the Bristly Ridge. The jagged spur, which affords an excellent scramble, plummets to Bwlch Tryfan.

This brings us to my favourite mountain, Tryfan, a magnificent wedge-shaped peak, slightly out on a limb from the main ridge. It towers over Ogwen, proudly boasting its buttresses and gullies to all who venture along the A5

Glyders - 1 Nant Peris to Y Garn

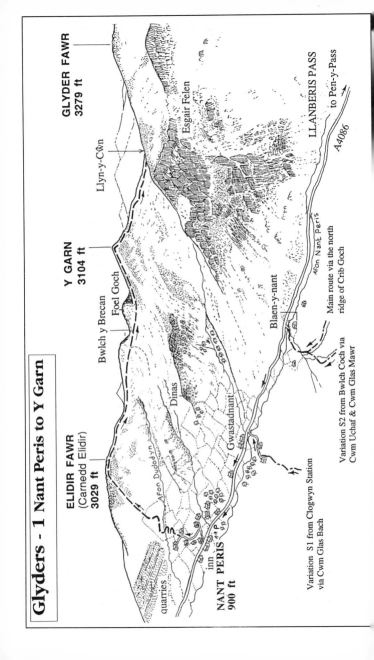

GLYDER FAWR
3279 ft

Y GARN
3104 ft

ELIDIR FAWR
(Carnedd Elidir)
3029 ft

NANT PERIS
900 ft

Foel Goch

Bwlch y Brecan

Esgair Felen

Llyn-y-Cŵn

LLANBERIS PASS
to Pen-y-Pass

A4086

Main route via the north
ridge of Crib Goch

Blaen-y-nant

Afon Nant Peris

Dinas

Gwastadnant

Afon Dudodyn

inn   P

quarries

Variation S1 from Clogwyn Station
via Cwm Glas Bach

Variation S2 from Bwlch Coch via
Cwm Uchaf & Cwm Glas Mawr

highway to Holyhead. Its sheer rock is impressive from every angle.

Standing on the shores of Llyn Ogwen, you cannot fail to be impressed by the bold facade of the mountain on the western skyline. Translated aptly as The Eminence, Y Garn certainly exudes nobility. It is strange to discover, however, that it has a soft side, for once on the summit you can see its grassy southern slopes declining gently towards Nant Peris. In fact, with the exception of Esgair Felin, which towers above the bouldered gorge of the Pass of Llanberis, the southern slopes of all the Glyders are more gentle than their northern counterparts.

The southern slopes of Elidir Fawr (Carnedd Elidir) have, been scarred by the vast quarries of Dinorwig to reveal stepped terraces of bare rock and barren slag heaps. This conical hill, the most remote of the three thousands, holds secrets, for hidden inside it are the workings of a pump-storage power station. The 1680MW station, which is built into the mountainside by the shores of Llyn Peris, was opened in 1984 at a cost of £450 million. It was then the largest of its type in the world. At times of peak demand for electricity (e.g. at breakfast) water from the Marchlyn Mawr Reservoir is released through tunnels 2000 foot down to power the six turbines. At times of low demand the turbines are reversed and water is pumped back up to Marchlyn Mawr, thus restoring levels, which can vary by over 150 feet.

The Glyderau – the route
Nant Peris to Idwal Cottage (Ogwen Valley)
Distance 9 miles (14.5 km)

The next stage of the route leaves **Nant Peris** via a walled lane, sandwiched between the chapel and campsite. After about 200yds/m, a footpath signpost points the way left along the narrow lane past the whitewashed cottage of Cerrig Dryddion to **Nant yr Fron**, which now belongs to a climbers' club.

Just beyond the latter, a stile to the right marks the start of the climb to Elidir Fawr. Here strike uphill by a stone

Foel Goch and Bwlch y Brecan (pass) from Elidir Fawr

barn to a ladder stile in the top corner of the pasture. Beyond the stile the path continues through an iron gate, where it zigzags uphill in delightful fields of bracken and foxgloves to reach a footbridge (GR 608596). Elidir Fawr lies directly ahead, its quarry-scarred, grassy facade soaring from the Afon Dudodyn *(water source)* to its craggy crest.

Leave the path to cross the bridge and continue on a tortuous slog northwards on a sketchy path climbing a crag-interspersed, grassy spur. After scaling a stile over a fence and the adjacent cross-wall it is best to rake across the grassy slopes towards the summit. Three erosion control fences have been erected in this vicinity but there are gaps quite close to the line of the old path. At about 2000ft (610m) you can usually feel the breezes from the col ahead, and soon the view opens out to reveal Foel Goch and Y Garn across the deep and desolate hollow of the Afon Dudodyn. The fragmented crest of Esgair Felen overshadows the cleft of the Llanberis Pass.

A vigorous final assault on **Elidir Fawr** now begins over boulder-ridden slopes to its hard won summit. Decorated by a comforting wind-shelter this is a fine place to linger if you're not racing against the clock. To the north-west, beyond Marchlyn Bach and its craggy amphitheatre, lie Bangor and the Menai Straits, framed by a flat, chequered pastureland speckled with trees, houses and rivers. To the south all but the very top of Snowdon is shielded by the arm of Clogwyn.

Leave Elidir's summit in a north-easterly direction in an initially rocky descent, aided by a few cairns. This soon transforms into a broad path on a grassy ridge, which, in turn, narrows into a rocky ridge with steep drops to the left. Marchllyn Mawr is framed beautifully from here – quite a spectacle if you are partial to nature being corrupted by symmetrical concrete shorelines. The route arcs round the grassy chasm of Cwm Dudodyn to **Bwlch y Brecan**, south of Mynydd Perfedd. Here you can look down over the deep valley of Nant Ffrancon, which divides the Glyderau from the Carneddau. The precipitous rugged slopes of Pen yr Ole Wen give a hint of the challenge yet to come.

Those in a hurry will choose to omit Foel-goch. Fine peak though it is, it fails to reach that magic three thousand foot figure, and a good level path obliges by traversing the southern slopes, rejoining the ridge above Cwm Cywion.

Here Y Garn imposes itself. A cairned track across loose slaty slopes leads to **Y Garn's** summit, which boasts one of the finest views in Wales. The lakes of Llyn Peris, Ogwen, Bochlwyd, Idwal and Y Garn's own attendant tarn, Llyn Clyd, are all visible, studded in a rugged mountainscape that includes the serrated tops and tremendous cliffs of Glyders Fawr and Fach, and distinctive Tryfan.

From Y Garn there are initially two paths of descent towards Llyn y Cwn. One stays closer to the cliff edge. Both are usable and converge beyond a fence. As the path nears the desolate small tarn (**Llyn y Cwn**) the terrain becomes more boggy. Here the path is joined by a path that has come up from Ogwen and the Devil's Kitchen. It makes a good escape for the footsore and weary.

Passing the lake *(water source - last until Ogwen)* on the left bank, go round a rocky knoll before forging upwards towards Glyder Fawr. There are several ways but the best one begins slightly to the left of a stony gully. The slippery, shaly path, which is extremely dangerous in wintry conditions, eases in the later stages as it zigzags to the

Castell y Gwynt (Castle of the Winds) on Glyder Fach

barren plateau, eventually arriving at some jagged outcrops
– a particularly large one marks the summit of your sixth
three thousand footer.

The connecting path to Glyder Fach is a pleasant and
entertaining stroll. The proliferation of cairns makes navigation easy in clear conditions but a little confusing in hill
fog. The views down the Nameless Cwm to the left are
breathtaking as a huge wall of rock, Clogwyn Du, plunges
2000ft (610m) into a craggy abyss with Llyn Idwal basking
in its rugged cwm far below. On the opposite side, the
heather-clad, stony southern slopes of Glyder Fach decline
more gently to Llyn Cwmffynnon and Pen y Gwryd.

At Bwlch y Ddwy Glyder the route is confronted by
Castell y Gwynt (Castle of the Winds), a juxtaposition of
sharp rocks some 200ft (60m) in height. There's an escape
route to Pen y Pass from here. Practised scramblers can
tackle them directly. It is easier however to pass to the
right of them, although this does involve some loss of
height and some grappling with bouldery slopes.

You are now on **Glyder Fach's** summit plateau: another
that has been likened to a lunar landscape. The actual summit is formed by a massive jumble of boulders. Continuing
eastwards the route passes close to the Cantilever, a giant

Glyders - 2 Y Garn to Ogwen

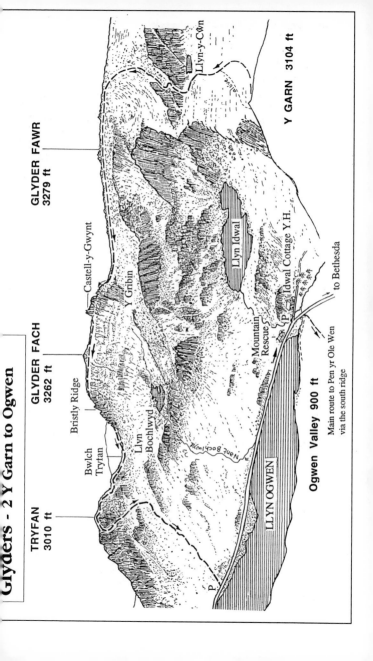

TRYFAN 3010 ft

GLYDER FACH 3262 ft

GLYDER FAWR 3279 ft

Y GARN 3104 ft

Bristly Ridge

Castell-y-Gwynt

Y Gribin

Bwlch Trytan

Llyn Bochlwyd

Llyn Idwal

Llyn-y-Cwn

Nant Bochlwyd

Mountain Rescue

P Idwal Cottage Y.H.

to Bethesda

Main route to Pen yr Ole Wen via the south ridge

Ogwen Valley 900 ft

LLYN OGWEN

P

slab precariously perched on a rock outcrop. On most occasions walkers will be posing for pictures.

Bearing north-east from the Cantilever, a large obtrusion of rock indicates the top of the Bristly Ridge and marks the start of the route to our eighth peak, Tryfan. **Bristly Ridge** itself is a time-consuming rock scramble and thus the best course is down the scree slopes to its right (east). They are steep and eroded and care should be taken, especially in snow or ice. Although Tryfan's triangular diadem, which now looms large before you, is not the highest of the Glyder peaks, it ranks as one of the finest in Wales.

From the pass, **Bwlch Tryfan**, scale any of the half-dozen stiles across a dry-stone wall. There are now two possible routes to the summit. Both involve a certain amount of easy scrambling: the path closest to the wall, although providing more shelter, introduces it at an earlier stage.

The two pillars on **Tryfan's** diminutive but airy summit are known as Adam and Eve. In the true traditions of temptation many walkers are coaxed into jumping the gap between the two rocks. Little is achieved. One slip though and a lot could be lost, so it's better to save your energies for the journey.

The steep descent from Tryfan is the one used in a popular fell race, where times of under seven minutes have been recorded from summit to the shores of Ogwen. A course should be set northwards towards a secondary peak.

On reaching the depression prior to this outpost, descend left (west) down a steep scree gully. At the bottom of the gully the path heads NNW down steep grassy slopes with the crest of the north ridge well to the right. The path meanders amongst grass and crag to reach Ogwen's shores via a roadside car park.

If you intend to use the "fast" route up Pen yr Ole Wen's south ridge, turn left along the road to Ogwen Cottage (Outdoor Centre) and Idwal Cottage Youth Hostel, where there are toilets, a refreshment kiosk and a car park. The opposite direction should be chosen for the more scenic east ridge.

THE CARNEDDAU

The Summits

Carnedd Llewelyn	3484 ft	(1064 m)
Carnedd Dafydd	3426 ft	(1044)
Pen yr Ole Wen	3210 ft	(978)
Foel Grach	3195 ft	(976)
Yr Elen	3152 ft	(962)
Foel Fras	3091 ft	(942)
Carnedd Uchaf	3038 ft	(926)

When approached on the A55 coast road to Conwy, the ruffled edge of Tal-y-fan signals the beginning of the high Carneddau. This remote range of mountains rises from the Irish Sea, spreading southwards into the heart of Snowdonia.

The Northern Carneddau consist of whaleback ridges and rounded hills, clad with pastel green tussocky grass, scattered with boulders and dissected by clear, cool mountain streams. In the loftier southern peaks rock

Carnedd Llewelyn and the Black Ladder cliffs

Carneddau - 1 Ogwen to Carnedd Llewelyn

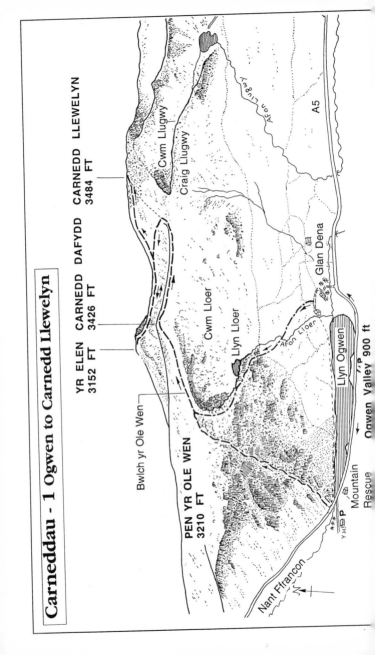

CARNEDD LLEWELYN
3484 FT

CARNEDD DAFYDD
3426 FT

YR ELEN
3152 FT

PEN YR OLE WEN
3210 FT

Bwlch yr Ole Wen

Cwm Llugwy

Craig Llugwy

Afon Llugwy

A5

Cwm Lloer

Llyn Lloer

Afon Lloer

Glan Dena

Llyn Ogwen

Ogwen Valley 900 ft

Mountain
Rescue

Nant Ffrancon

surfaces more frequently in the form of cliffs such as Carnedd Dafydd's Ysgolion Duon (the Black Ladders) and Craig yr Ysfa.

The tops are boulder strewn and interspersed with heather and bilberry. The last sentinel, Pen yr Ole Wen, watches over Ogwen where, in one swoop, craggy, scree-strewn slopes plummet over two thousand feet. Between north and south is an area as wild and remote as any in Snowdonia – one rather akin to the Cairngorms of Scotland.

In good weather the free-striding, broad ridges between Pen yr Ole Wen and Foel Fras are a delight, but route-finding can be difficult in misty conditions, especially in the region of Foel Grach. Judging by stories in the refuge shelter, many walkers have had narrow escapes.

For the Welsh Three Thousander, passing the refuge hut should herald the start of a triumphant period, taking those last steps in the fading evening light to the summit of Foel Fras.

The Carneddau – The Route
Ogwen to Foel Fras
Distance 9 miles (15 km)

Eclipsing Ogwen, the precipitous fortress of Pen yr Ole Wen mocks the aching limbs, which have just surrendered over two thousand feet on a descent from the Glyders. In the space of just a mile, all of that will have to be regained. Take heart, for once you have cracked this one the succeeding lofty Carneddau ridges will offer an easy-paced finale all the way to Foel Fras.

Go through the gap stile in the stone wall (GR 649606) just beyond the road bridge over the **Afon Ogwen** *(water source)*.

After clambering over a series of rock steps to a grassy terrace, a fairly prominent path climbs steeply to higher slopes, which are clad with heather and bilberry. This subsequently gives way to loose scree and an unrelenting slog, which is nevertheless made bearable by stunning views across Ogwen to Tryfan's North Ridge and Cwm Idwal.

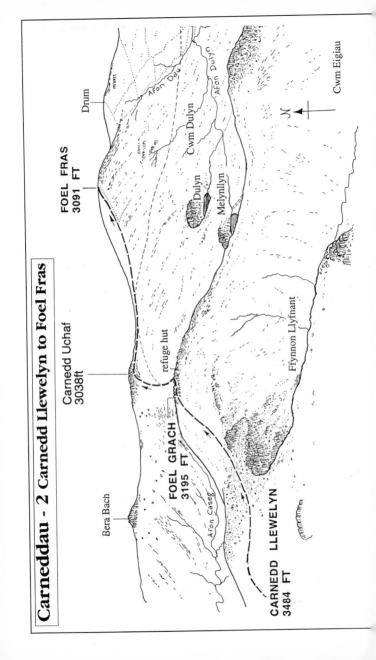

Carneddau - 2 Carnedd Llewelyn to Foel Fras

Drum

FOEL FRAS
3091 FT

Afon Ddu

Afon Dulyn

Cwm Dulyn

Dulyn

Melynllyn

Cwm Eigiau

Carnedd Uchaf
3038ft

refuge hut

Ffynnon Llyfnant

Bera Bach

FOEL GRACH
3195 FT

Afon Caseg

CARNEDD LLEWELYN
3484 FT

Snowdon appears over the top of the dark crags of the Devil's Kitchen.

Having been duped by a couple of false summits it is a relief to see the cairn and wind-shelter at the edge of **Pen yr Ole Wen's** large stony summit plateau. Now in northern vistas Carnedd Dafydd and Carnedd Llewelyn fill the frame, with lesser peaks guiding the eye to Anglesey and the North Wales coast.

After climbing a little farther across the large, grassy plateau to the summit, the path descends north-westwards to Bwlch yr Ole Wen. Here the delightful craggy arena of Cwm Lloer and its small tarn capture the attention.

Follow the edge of the cwm before climbing north-eastwards on an undulating ridge to **Carnedd Dafydd**, whose summit also boasts a cairn and useful wind-shelter.

The track descending from Carnedd Dafydd hugs the edge of Ysgolion Duon (the Black Ladders). These precipitous cliffs at the head of the barren valley of the Afon Llafar are popular with rock climbers in the summer and snow and ice climbers in the winter.

Carnedd Llewelyn, though highest of the Carneddau, is uninteresting from this vantage. Its massif now lies ahead, but the Welsh 3s route will first visit the shapely peak of Yr Elen to avoid scaling the former twice. This is done by contouring its southern slopes to the col above Cwm Caseg, where the pull to **Yr Elen** begins. En route you pass a spring *(water source)*. Being off the main ridge, this superb little peak is usually quiet.

Carnedd Llewelyn now looks like a real mountain, its rocky facade soaring above the shady depths of Cwm Caseg, whose diminutive tarn is an idyllic campsite.

After returning to the col by way of a serrated rocky ridge, the route tackles **Carnedd Llewelyn** using a good path at the edge of the cwm.

The path then veers to the right to attain the huge cairn and wind-shelter in the midst of a vast, stone-scattered, grassy summit plateau. Views have widened to encompass expansive stretches of the North Wales coastline and the chequered emerald fields of the Conwy Valley, which lie beyond the sprawling grassy hills of the Northern

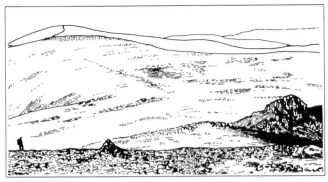

Descending Carnedd Llewelyn looking north to Foel Grach and Foel Fras

Carneddau.

The ridge between Carnedd Llewelyn and Foel Fras is wide and, although pleasant to follow in clear weather, can be extremely confusing in mist. Good compass skills are essential here! A cairned track descends NNE before a slight rise to the bouldered summit of **Foel Grach**. Slightly to the north of the summit, camouflaged beneath crags, is the Refuge Shelter, much maligned by some, who feel it is alien to the wildness of the mountain environment. This view would almost certainly not be shared by the travellers who have gratefully stumbled across it in adverse conditions and have left messages of relief in the shelter's log book.

The twin lakes of Melynllyn and Dulyn lie tantalisingly out of view beneath Foel Grach's concave slopes and dark crags. A time-consuming detour would have to be made to see them. Most will want to press on to **Carnedd Uchaf** (the latest three thousander after re-surveying). Its stony top is gained with minimum effort. The terrain becomes increasingly less stony as the climb to our last peak, **Foel Fras** begins. From GR 695677 a stone ridge-wall guides you to the summit trig point. Somehow the dull top seems an unfitting climax to such a classic walk. However the solitude of this northern outpost allows quiet contemplation of the day's triumphs.

ROUTES BACK TO CIVILISATION

For those with friends to pick them up by car:

1) To Bwlch Y Ddeufaen (GR 721716)

Distance - 4 miles (6 km)

Continue along the ridge (aided by a fence) over Drum (pronounced Drim), Carnedd y Ddelw and Drosgl to reach the Roman Road. Turn right to the terminus of the motor road half a mile distant.

2) To lane beneath Penygadair (GR 744694)

Distance - 4 miles (6 km)

Continue along the ridge to intersection of fences (GR 704685). Descend (trackless) by fence to meet right of way, which should then followed north-east beneath Pen y Castell and Penygadair to the road.

For the 'loners':

3) To Aber

Distance - 6 miles (10 km)

A much longer walk. Follow the ridge to Drum where a rough vehicle track leads to the old Roman Road at GR

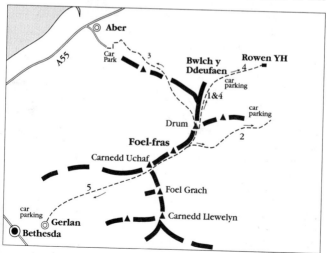

693722. Turn left along the old road, which becomes surfaced and follows the wooded lower valley of the Anafon to Bont Newydd before continuing to the village of Aber. (Coastal bus service.)

4) To Rowen Youth Hostel (GR 747721)
Distance - 5 miles (8 km)
Follow route 1 for Bwlch y Ddeufaen and take the left fork in the lanes at GR 732715.

5) To Gerlan/ Bethesda
Distance - 5 miles (8 km)
Retrace steps back towards Carnedd Uchaf. Before reaching its summit, take the path which threads between this and Yr Aryg. A descent is then made on grassy slopes into Cwm Caseg, where a well-marked track leads to the head of the lane at GR 639665.

Route Variations

Snowdon

Variation S1
From Pen-y-Pass via Crib Goch - See map Page 24

Although not accepted for record purposes, this route is probably the fastest of all. Follow the Pig Track to Bwlch y Moch but instead of going into Cwm Dyli turn right onto Crib Goch's steep, rocky flanks.

The route is initially cairned but more often than not you can see walkers floundering at the foot of a crag. There are plenty of hand and footholds however and the difficulty is short-lived. The route continues on slaty slopes to Crib Goch's exposed top. The route to the summits of Carnedd Ugain and Yr Wyddfa is the reverse of the previously described 3000's route.

From Snowdon, the Llanberis Path is used initially on the descent but it is abandoned by the railway bridge (GR 608561) near Clogwyn Station for a precipitous and spectacular descent into Cwm Glas Bach. Initially the route descends a series of grass steps before continuing along a rocky groove, raking left below the impressive cliffs of Llechog. The route now drops down a scree gully towards a stream. On reaching the stream *(water source)*, it deviates left to avoid rock ledges above the water's edge. From here the path becomes sketchy as it twists round crags and over steep, grassy slopes with a rocky spur to the left. The combination of short grass and an acute angle of descent make the terrain hereabouts very slippery after wet weather. Views across the valley to the Glyders are impressive.

After going through a gap in a drystone wall (GR 611570) head north-eastwards for some sheepfolds before veering left and passing the front of the Cwm Glas Bach Cottage, avoiding the house. Here an access lane* leads through a gate and over a bridge spanning the Afon Nant Peris to the road at Gwastadnant. A left turn is then made into Nant Peris, half a mile distant.

* Please note that the lane is a negotiated courtesy route to the access area beneath Carnedd Ugain: be considerate.

Variation S2
Descent of Crib Goch via Bwlch Goch – See map page 24

Although this means retracing steps to **Bwlch Goch**, the pass between Crib Goch and Carnedd Ugain, the route can be marginally faster than the descent via the North Ridge. This variation was used by Colin Donnelly in his record run of 1988.

The key to the route is to descend the steep, scree-strewn flanks northwards into **Cwm Uchaf**. From Bwlch Goch, many try to contour the easier slopes to the left beneath Clogwyn y Person, but consequently find themselves with crags and cliffs to negotiate. From the marshy bowl of Cwm Uchaf a continuation is made along the eastern banks of the stream *(water source)* that drains its tiny pools. The path, which varies between faint and non-existent, descends, threading through crags and bluffs into Cwm Glas Mawr, where you ford the stream. After traversing marshy grasslands and fording two more streams (GRs 618562 & 617563), the route joins a well-defined stony

The S2 descent from Crib Goch to Llyn Glas

path. This descends close to the western banks of the main stream, passing the cottage of **Blaen-y-nant** before recrossing the stream via a wooden footbridge. After crossing another bridge, this time over the Afon Nant Peris, the road is met and followed to the left into Nant Peris.

N.B: It is possible to vary the route from Cwm Uchaf by heading NW over grassy flanks to Llyn Glas *(water source)*, a beautiful tarn set beneath the imposing cliffs of Clogwyn y Person. The eastern banks of the tarn are traced before turning right opposite its island. Soon after descending stony flanks a footpath becomes evident. It descends bouldery slopes close to the western banks of a stream (GR 619560) before joining the previously mentioned route beneath the cliffs in the marshy environs of Cwm Glas Mawr.

The Glyderau

There are few variations available on the Glyderau. Experienced mountaineers in no hurry could scramble down Glyder Fach's Bristly Ridge then down Tryfan's spiky north ridge (both better in ascent than descent and more suitable to a north to south traverse). Another feasible route would be to retrace steps from the summit of Tryfan to Bwlch Tryfan and then take the path down to Llyn Bochlwyd, one of the range's many delightful tarns. A well-used path continues down to Ogwen Cottage.

The Carneddau

Variation C1
Pen Yr Ole Wen via its East Ridge – See map page 36

Although not quite as quick as the south ridge route, this delightful alternative is definitely for the connoisseur, offering fine views over Ffynnon Lloer.

The route begins at GR 668605, a short distance east of Llyn Ogwen. A public footpath points northwards to a gravel track that dissects a small fir plantation and passes **Glan Dena**, the Midland Mountaineers Association's cottage. Just before reaching the farm, the track is abandoned for a path to the right, which follows a wall northwards to a ladder stile. The stile is scaled and an intermittent path strikes northwards uphill by the Afon Lloer *(water source)*. The stream should be crossed at GR 667612. From here the path continues over ground, which can be boggy after periods of heavy rain. The gradient steepens on approaching the intake wall (at the border of pasture-land and mountainside) and a stile (GR 667617) by a gate is scaled. An indistinct path (ENE) now leads to the higher ground of the east ridge. A large crag appears to bar the way. Closer examination reveals a gully and an easy scramble up it gains the ridge where a delightful path climbs over heather and crag with a sudden view into the exquisite Cwm Lloer and its gem of a tarn. Views of the Glyders are enlivened by the wedge of Tryfan and Glyder Fawr. The latter overlooks the Devil's Kitchen, a rugged defile high on a rocky shelf above Cwm Idwal.

In the final stages the stony path hugs the edge of the cwm before leading westwards to **Pen yr Ole Wen's**

Carnedd Llewelyn as seen from Yr Elen.

summit cairn, where it meets the main route to Carnedd Dafydd.

The 3000's North to South

Although the majority of walkers will start on Snowdon and end with the tranquillity of Foel Fras, some will prefer to tackle the route in reverse. The most obvious benefit from a north to south crossing is the fitting climax on the highest ground, Yr Wyddfa. If a fast time is combined with an early start you will be afforded the luxury of a pint at the summit hotel and the possibility of using the Snowdon Railway down to Llanberis. The descent from Snowdon to Llanberis is far safer in the fading light than the less frequented Carneddau tracks from Foel Fras.

Each itinerary has its appeal. The stiff climbs up Tryfan, Glyder Fach and Crib Goch's north ridge are far less intimidating in ascent than in descent and that slog to Elidir Fawr from Nant Peris becomes a pleasant way down. Conversely the steep, scree-strewn descent from Pen yr Ole Wen to Ogwen becomes a real knee-trembler.

The fastest way to get to the summit of Foel Fras is to get transport to GR 721715 at the terminus of the Bwlch y Ddeufaen road, then climb Drosgl's north-eastern ridge to Drum and thence to Foel Fras. An alternative start is from the Bont Newydd Car Park at Aber (GR 662720). If somebody is giving you a lift they can take you to the end of the lane at GR 676714. Here a stony track is used to climb to Drum, turning right at the crossroads (GR 693722) between Garreg Fawr and Foel Ganol. Ignore the track to Llyn Anafon unless you fancy a steep climb out to the col between Drum and Foel Fras.

A swift pace can be adopted on the gentle Carneddau gradients but, in mist, route finding is difficult on the broad and featureless ridges, especially in the regions between Foel Fras and Carnedd Uchaf.

Be careful not to be enticed on the short cut path from the pass between the two, for this heads directly for Foel Grach, missing out the latter peak. As with the south to

north route, Carnedd Llewelyn need only be scaled once.
This is achieved by contouring its south western flanks
after leaving Yr Elen. Carnedd Dafydd is gained with little
difficulty, as is Pen yr Ole Wen. In descent, the east ridge is
more pleasant, although slightly slower than the direct
southern face. It also avoids those precipitous gradients
and loose screes encountered throughout the descent to
Ogwen.

The simplest way up Tryfan is the route described in the
main itinerary, beginning from the car park at GR 658603.
Although steep, its course is never in doubt. An entertaining but more time-consuming alternative would be to
scramble up the craggy North Ridge route followed by
Bristly Ridge to Glyder Fach.

From Tryfan it's a clamber down to Bwlch Tryfan then
up the screes to the east of Bristly Ridge to Glyder Fach,
where the route continues over a chaotic boulder-strewn
plateau to Castell y Gwynt.

If you are familiar with the area you will be able to
scramble directly down the rocky buttress but otherwise
it would be prudent to detour to the left (this means los-
ing a fair bit of height and still requires some boulder-hop-
ping). It's a straightforward cairned path to Glyder Fawr,
although the drop to Llyn y Cwn requires care, its shaly
and friable surface makes the going difficult in places,
especially in wintry conditions. From Llyn y Cwn the terrain is mainly grassy, except for the summit apex of Y
Garn – one of the finest viewpoints in Snowdonia if you
have time to stop.

Foel Goch is the next summit in line but it is avoided by
a path that maintains a level course on its south-western
slopes to reach Bwlch y Brecan. Here the assault on Elidir
Fawr begins, contouring around Cwm Dudodyn before
climbing a rocky spur which leads to this last Glyder summit.

After scrambling over boulders, an easy descent ensues
over grassy slopes southwards to cross the Afon Dudodyn
at a footbridge (GR 608596). The path then zigzags down
fields dappled with bracken and foxgloves, to reach a
country lane by the cottage of Nant-yr-Fron. This leads to

the village of Nant Peris at the foot of Snowdon. Refreshments await at the Vaynol Arms.

You are now on the last leg but it is a real grind up the tarmac road to Blaen-y-nant Farm. Crib Goch just towers above – it's a sting in the tail and a nasty sting at that. The paths ascending Crib Goch from here are far less frequented than others on the Snowdon range and present a stiff navigational test in the middle regions (where most peter out into sheep tracks). Initially the stony path from the cottage is good. It climbs by the rushing stream towards Cwm Glas Mawr but is left to cross the stream, aiming for a cleft in the craggy hillslopes to the left (GR 622562). Clamber up the left side of the falls, which cascade through the cleft, then over a wide path on the steep red screes to Crib Goch's north ridge. From here it's exposed ridges all the way – first to Crib Goch's summit, then over the Pinnacles to Bwlch Goch before the pull to Carnedd Ugain. Be careful not to be misled by paths which lead too far down the southern flanks above Glaslyn. From Carnedd Ugain's broad summit plateau it's plain sailing. If you've got this far the final slog following the path to the left of the Snowdon Railway will provide little resistance and there's always the thought of making it to the cafe before closing time (generally 5pm)!

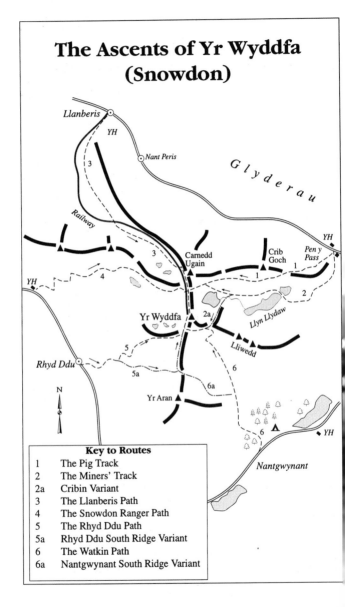

The Ascents of Yr Wyddfa (Snowdon)

Key to Routes

1	The Pig Track
2	The Miners' Track
2a	Cribin Variant
3	The Llanberis Path
4	The Snowdon Ranger Path
5	The Rhyd Ddu Path
5a	Rhyd Ddu South Ridge Variant
6	The Watkin Path
6a	Nantgwynant South Ridge Variant

Getting to the Top of Snowdon

The main Welsh Three Thousands route begins at the summit. Many make the ascent by train but it's expensive. I have therefore listed descriptions of the main routes to the summit. All are well used and should, in good conditions, be easily discernible underfoot.

Route 1 - The Pig Track

Distance	3 miles (5.1 km)
Ascent	2400 ft (740m)
Start	Pen y Pass, GR 648557
Difficulty	Moderate
Time	2-3 hrs up; 2 hours in descent

Sometimes incorrectly referred to as the Pyg Track after the Pen y Gwryd Hotel, this route actually takes its name from Bwlch y Moch (Pass of the Pigs). It's the most scenic of the popular routes up Snowdon and one of the quicker ones.

The Pig Track begins from the Pen y Pass through a gap in the wall at the top of the car park. A flagged path blasts its way through rocky outcrops above the Pass of Llanberis with the imposing peak of Crib Goch dominating views ahead. The path veers left to Bwlch Moch, where spectacular views of Cwm Dyli appear with the cliffs of Lliwedd soaring from Llyn Llydaw.

The route now skirts the lower southern slopes of Crib Goch, climbing to a second higher cwm. Here the blue-green waters of Glaslyn lie cradled by the slopes of Yr Wyddfa, Carnedd Ugain and the rocky spur of Y Gribin. The path continues across loose and fragile terrain to reach the infamous zigzags, a robustly constructed stairway that climbs to Bwlch Glas, the pass between Yr Wyddfa and Carnedd Ugain. On reaching the obelisk at the pass, turn left, tracing the cliff's edge parallel to the line of the Snowdon Railway to the summit. Many people follow the course of the railway to the summit but this can be dangerous and unnecessary as the path hereabouts has now been improved.

Route 2 The Miners' Track

Distance   3½ miles (5.8 km)
Ascent   2400 feet (740 m)
Start   Pen y Pass, GR 648557
Difficulty   very easy to Glaslyn then steep pull to
              the summit
Time   2-3 hours up: 2 hours in descent

This utilises part of an old copper miners' route connecting Bethesda with the Glaslyn Mine at the foot of Yr Wyddfa. Like the Pig Track it is very scenic, offering fine views of Cwm Dyli and its cliffs.

The wide, stony track from the left hand side of the Pen y Pass car park takes the route past Llyn Teyrn into Cwm Dyli. This vast hollow is filled by the expansive waters of Llyn Llydaw. The lake is crossed by way of a causeway and the stony track continues along its northern shores, passing the derelict crushing mill.

Beyond Llyn Llydaw the track climbs more steadily from the

On Yr Wyddfa, the highest of Snowdon's peaks

foot of Crib Goch to the shores of Glaslyn, a small tarn tightly enclosed by the mighty slopes of Yr Wyddfa and Carnedd Ugain and cradled by the rocky spur of Y Gribin. At the termination of the track, beyond the ruins of the old mine barracks, the gentle nature of the walk ceases. A cairned path struggles over loose, stony slopes leading to the Pig Track, which zigzags to the obelisk at Bwlch Glas. From here a left turn takes you by the railway to the summit.

Variant 2a - Scramble up Y Gribin

For experienced mountain walkers the scamble up the Gribin ridge offers one of the most exciting ways up Snowdon.

It leaves the Miners Track just short of Llyn Glaslyn to cross the outflow of the lake (not recommended after heavy rain). Keep to the crest of the ridge using the plentiful hand-holds in firm rock. After steepening in the later stages, the route achieves the ridge near Bwlch y Saethau (pass of the arrows), where it meets and follows the Watkin Path (route 6) to the summit of Snowdon.

This is not recommended as a route of descent.

Route 3 - The Llanberis Path

Distance	5 miles (8 km)
Ascent	3200 feet (980 m)
Start	Llanberis GR 583597
Difficulty	Easy but long. Can be awkward in winter
Time	3 hours up: 2 hours in descent.

The easiest and most popular ascent of Snowdon, the Llanberis path begins on a tarmac lane opposite the Royal Victoria Hotel. The lane climbs steeply before being abandoned for a signposted footpath to the left. The Snowdon Mountain Railway is never far away and provides a little interest on a relatively dull climb on the spur of Llechog, which rises from the valley of the Afon Arddu. Halfway House (GR 599569), which once provided refreshments now lies derelict, but there are plans to re-open it. Beyond Clogwyn Station the path cuts under the railway, revealing superb lofty views of the Pass of Llanberis.

The route steepens as it veers southwards, traversing the shoulder of Carnedd Ugain past the monolith at Bwlch Glas,

where there are exquisite views down Cwm Dyli, and finally
to the summit.

Route 4 - The Snowdon Ranger Path

Distance	3½ miles (5.8 km)
Ascent	3000 feet (930m)
Start	The Snowdon Ranger Youth Hostel, Betws Garmon, GR 565551
Difficulty	moderate
Time	2-3 hours up: 2 hours in descent

This is probably the least used of the Snowdon routes and,
although not the most spectacular, it does have its moments. It
is also probably the safest route in the Winter months.

Zigzagging across rough, grassy slopes the path gives fine
views towards Moel Hebog and the Nantlle Ridge, which lie
invitingly across the sparkling waters of Llyn y Gader.

As the path gains height the scene becomes more dramatic
with Llyn Ffynnon-y-gwas nestling in the sullen, crag-ringed
bowl of Cwm Clogwyn. Once it reaches Bwlch Cwm Brwynog,
the going gets harder and now snakes up the rocky arm of
Clogwyn Du'r Arddu.

Where the gradients ease, bear left to gain views of the cliffs
of Clogwyn Du'r Arddu, a favoured spot for experienced
climbers. It's now a simple ascent over the stony shoulder of
Carnedd Ugain to reach the mountain railway, where a monolith marks the spot. Cross the railway and continue to Bwlch
Glas. Here the path follows the crest of the ridge to the left
(east) of the railway to Snowdon's summit.

Route 5 - The Rhyd Ddu Path

Distance	4 miles (6 km)
Ascent	2950 feet (910m)
Start	Car Park (with toilets), Rhyd Ddu GR 571526
Difficulty	quite easy
Time	3 hours up: 2 hours in descent

This interesting, if unspectacular route begins on a quarry road
to the north of the large car park. At GR 583525 the road,
which heads for Bwlch Cwm y Llan between Yr Wyddfa and Yr

Aran, is abandoned. A path to the left, beyond a gate, now wends its way amongst rocky outcrops to attain the Llechog ridge, where dark cliffs plummet in a spectacular scene to Cwm Clogwyn.

A gravelly path winds steeply uphill to Bwlch Main where you overlook the gigantic hollow of Cwm Tregalan towards the stony western flanks of Y Lliwedd. From Bwlch Main the path climbs steadily on a rocky ridge NNE passing the station and cafe en route to the summit.

Variation 5a via the South Ridge

At GR 583525 continue along the quarry road to Bwlch Cwm y Llan then head northwards on Yr Wyddfa's southern ridge to meet the Rhyd-Ddu route on Bwlch Main.

Route 6 - The Watkin Path

Distance	4 miles (6.4 km)
Ascent	3400 feet (1045m)
Start	Lay-by car park, Pont Bethania, GR 628506
Difficulty	More ascent and tougher than other routes
Time	3-4 hours up: 3 hours down.

The path takes its name from Sir Edward Watkin, a wealthy railway owner who engineered it as a donkey track. It was opened by Gladstone in 1892.

Take the narrow tarmac northbound lane opposite the lay-by but leave it for a signposted path on the left, which winds into the beautiful glen of the Afon Llan. After passing some impressive waterfalls, the path climbs into Cwm Llan dominated by the huge precipices of Craig Ddu, with the Snowdon massif forming the background. Cross the stream by the ruins of Plas Cwm y Llan, once a quarry manager's house.

On reaching Gladstone Rock, the route veers westwards to circumvent Craig Ddu. It then climbs to the barren Cwm Tregalan, which is hemmed in by the ramparts of Yr Wyddfa and Y Lliwedd. After passing the ruined barracks and spoil heaps of another slate quarry, the Watkin Path heads north-east out of the cwm. In the upper reaches it zigzags over the stony wilderness of Lliwedd's western flanks to attain Bwlch Ciliau, overlooking Cwm Dyli and its huge lake, Llyn Llydaw. There are wonderful views of Yr Wyddfa (L) together with the bold dark cliffs of Lliwedd (R) which look across to the Crib Goch - Crib y Ddysgl ridge.

You have now joined the 'horseshoe' route. A wide path aims north-west for Bwlch y Saethau along a fairly level, airy ridge.

Beyond the bwlch, the ascent to Yr Wyddfa's summit is steep and care should be exercised. There are two paths – one heading directly along the edge for the summit and the other raking left to join the Rhyd-Ddu path on the South Ridge by a stone obelisk. Both climb over horribly loose, shaly slopes, which can be treacherous, but the latter is the easier and safer course.

Variation 6a via Bwlch Cwm y Llan & the South Ridge

Less crowded than the Watkin Path, this variant also avoids the treacherous screes on the final pull to the summit. There is still much ascent and it's quite arduous.

Turn left from the Watkin Path at GR 622520, just before it crosses the river, and climb to the old quarry tramway, which is followed to GR 617521. A path from here climbs to Bwlch Cwm y Llan, a pass between Yr Wyddfa and Yr Aran. Yr Wyddfa's south ridge is then followed to the summit.

The Snowdon Horseshoe

by Roy Clayton

Distance: 8 miles (13km)
Ascent 3400ft (1000m)
Time: 8 hours

The Snowdon Horseshoe is one of the finest ridge walks in Europe. It takes the description "ridge" to the limit, for tracks in some places become non existent as the foot-moulded razor-edged crests tumble into the valleys, leaving the walker exposed and occasionally uneasy.

In wintry conditions, the Horseshoe is a very serious mountaineering exercise and, sadly, claims many lives. It should not be attempted by anyone not equipped with and proficient in the use of both crampons and an ice axe.

Most people start the walk from Pen y Pass youth hostel and make for Crib Goch on the Pig Track but I think that to do it in the reverse order is better. Firstly the loose upper sections of the Watkin Path are much easier when climbing and secondly, I think the prospects from the Crib Goch – Crib-y-ddysgl Ridge are more interesting when seen from this direction.

Take the 8ft wide Miners' Track from the left hand side of the car park (GR 648557) heading in a southerly direction. A good pace can be maintained over the path, which gains little height at first.

After a quarter of a mile the track veers to the right, exposing the sheer cliffs of Y Lliwedd and, in the mid-distance, the conical peak of Y Wyddfa. To the right and looking equally magnificent are the quartz-banded ramparts of Crib Goch.

The path continues past the derelict copper-mining cottages overlooking Llyn Teyrn, a small tarn secretly set in a grassy hollow amongst small bluffs. It then climbs out of the hollow to a corrugated iron shed on the shores of Llyn Llydaw, a much larger lake that occupies the vast chasm of Cwm Dyli. Here, leave

Walker on the Crib Goch Pinnacles with Yr Wyddfa in the background

the old Miners' Track, which blasts a course up Cwm Dyli. The horseshoe route bears left along the southern shores of Llyn Llydaw and crosses a metal footbridge before striking uphill at a moderate gradient. A twenty foot dip precedes an area of slightly boggy flat ground, which offers brief respite before the collar work commences on an arduous ascent towards Lliwedd. The stony track gains height rapidly as it weaves around a series of rock ledges to attain the ridge by a large cairn (GR 631535) to the north east of Lliwedd Bach. Although the majesty of Snowdon and its satellites dominates, it is pleasing to see the contrasting softer scenery contained in the wide sweep of Nantgwynant to the south. Its shimmering lakes and pastures are patched with woodland and fringed with the gritty knolls of the Moelwyn-Siabod ridge.

The route now continues along the cliff-edge to Lliwedd Bach. This will be remembered for its secret niches offering views of the dark precipices of both East and West Lliwedd, which tower a thousand feet above Llyn Llydaw. The bouldery cairned path keeps close to the edge before clambering over both the Lliwedd summits. From the top of the west summit

The Snowdon Horseshoe

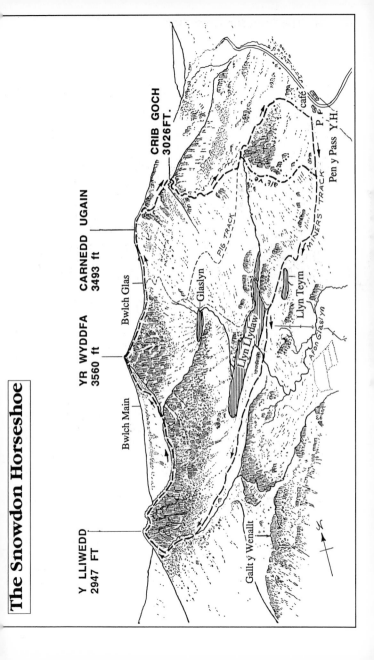

Y LLIWEDD 2947 FT

YR WYDDFA 3560 ft

CARNEDD UGAIN 3493 ft

CRIB GOCH 3026FT.

Bwlch Main

Bwlch Glas

Glaslyn

PIG TRACK

Llyn Llydaw

Llyn Teyrn

Afon Glaslyn

Gallt y Wenallt

MINERS TRACK

Pen y Pass Y.H.

café

P.P.

PYG TRACK

Yr Wyddfa seen across the waters of Llyn Llydaw

Glaslyn is glimpsed over the rocky spur of Y Gribin.

The path now descends on heavily bouldered slopes to Bwlch Ciliau, where it's joined by the popular Watkin Path to Y Wyddfa's summit. Continue along the ridge to Bwlch y Saethau (pass of the arrows) where the Snowdon summit massif casts its shadow. There is a wonderful retrospective view down the length of Cwm Dyli, taking in Crib y Ddysgl, Crib Goch and the latter part of the Horseshoe.

There is a confusing network of paths at the pass, including one that descends the spur of Y Gribin and some that just visit the edge above Glaslyn. In mist it is best to stick to the main route, which now keeps below and left of the crest of the ridge, overlooking the vast hollow of Cwm Tregalan. The final stages of the route to Y Wyddfa's summit can be tricky for its flanks are steep and the shaly surface rock friable. Two paths exist. The one to the right aims for the summit directly, but is not recommended. The correct route slants left across the slippery southern slopes. It climbs steeply, twisting and turning in its quest to find an easy way, but finally it attains the southern ridge by a huge monolith. Here the Watkin Path and the Rhyd Ddu Path meet for a joint onslaught on the summit. Looking westwards, the impressive peaks of the Nantlle Ridge and Mynydd Mawr form the backdrop to Rhyd Ddu and the nearby lakes of Cwellyn, Gader and Dywarchen.

It's now just a short easy climb to Yr Wyddfa's summit, passing the cafe en route. The summit cairn is usually swarming with tourists, many of whom have made the journey on the mountain railway. They will share with you one of the great panoramas of Europe. Although not of alpine proportions, the view from Snowdon reveals magnificent glacial architecture in a labyrinth of cwms, aretes and buttresses. In good conditions half of Wales can be seen – its coastline, distant towns and range upon range of mountains paling to the horizon.

The route from the summit to Crib Goch is identical to that described in the Welsh 3000's. Briefly, it descends to Bwlch Glas close to Cwm Dyli's edge and parallel to the railway before the easy climb to Carnedd Ugain. From here follow the crest of the ridge on a tricky course over Crib y Ddysgl to Bwlch Goch before the final airy assault on Crib Goch and its infamous 'Pinnacles'. The descent from Crib Goch is tricky, especially in snow and ice. It begins with an airy passage over shaly slopes eastwards towards Bwlch Moch. This terrain ends abruptly at a rocky ledge, where good hand and footholds help the way down to a cairned track, which winds more sedately down the steep lower slopes to meet the Pig Track at Bwlch Moch. The newly renovated track is somewhat overdone and unsympathetic to its surroundings. To be fair, time and a million boots will subdue it, and it does offer a quick way back to base at Pen y Pass. It also has good views of the harsh boulder-strewn Pass of Llanberis and the rocky crest of Esgair Felen.

The Welsh 1000 Metres Race
(Snowdonia Summits Marathon)

After the Second World War the Welch Fusiliers, clad in full battle dress, used the Welsh Three Thousands as a training exercise. As numbers grew they were accused of contributing to
the severe erosion on the mountainside and pressure was put
on them to find an alternative. They chose the 'One
Thousands', a route which visits the four Snowdonian peaks
that top 1000m in elevation – i.e. Yr Wyddfa and Carnedd
Ugain from the Snowdon Group and Carnedds Llewelyn and
Dafydd from the Carneddau.

THE ROUTE Aber to Snowdon
Distance: 19 miles (31 km) - current route.
Ascent: 8900 feet (2700 metres)
Control points are listed in brackets.

Shorter than the Welsh Three Thousands, this route begins on
the seashore at Aber (GR 649732) between Conwy and Bangor.
It passes southwards through the village and enters the wooded glen of the Afon Rhaeadr Fawr (river of the big waterfall). It
leaves the main track to the Aber Falls to enter into the darkness of pine woods to the east before emerging in the open by
some expansive scree slopes. Beyond the scree slopes a tricky
but short wet rock section leads to the top of the falls. Here
the impressive spout plummets a couple of hundred feet over a
rocky precipice and the walker (or runner without the speed
or inclination to win races) can look back across the lip to
Anglesey and Puffin Island.

The route now enters the wild inner sanctum of the
Carneddau via the remote hanging valley of the Afon Goch
where sheeptracks trace the east banks of the river (*water
source*). Two rocky crests, Lwytmor and Bera Mawr, stand
either side of the valley like sentries. The paths gets fainter

Leaving the forest to approach Aber Falls near the beginning of the race

until they disappear among tussocky grasses at the head of the cwm. Climb out to join the main Carneddau ridge between Foel Fras (left) and Carnedd Uchaf (right).

A well-defined path leads over the rocky summit of Carnedd Uchaf before tackling the steep grass slopes to Foel Grach's boulder-ridden top. Amongst the boulders on its north-east flanks there is a mountain refuge hut, which is useful for those caught out in a storm. Unfortunately, it has on too many occasions been used as a place for the ill-mannered to dump their surplus orange peel and Coke cans.

The ridge broadens as it swells to the first 1000 metre peak, **Carnedd Llewelyn (control L)**. Prince Llewelyn's cairn looks down on that of his little brother, Dafydd, while Snowdon and the pointed Elidir Fawr form a backdrop.

The well-used path descends to a col separating the hollows of Cwm Lugwy and Cwm Pen-llafr. The views are channelled down to Bethesda, a village surrounded by the piles of discarded slate.

Ysgolion Duon, the Black Ladders, are gigantic climbers' cliffs that seldom see the sun. The route stays close on its way up the stony slopes to **Carnedd Dafydd (D)**. Another peak, Pen yr Ole Wen, lies to the south but it doesn't reach the

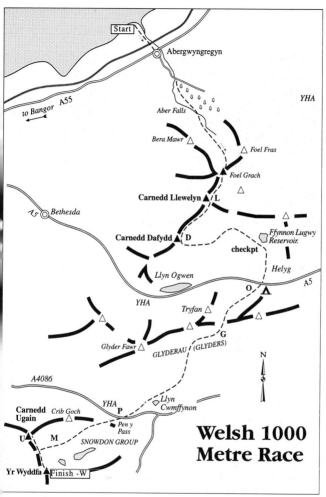

Welsh 1000 Metre Race

required metric figure, so the 1000s turns up its nose and ignores this upstart.

Originally a descent was made directly from Carnedd Dafydd down to Ogwen, but due to access problems this has been changed. The new, more circuitous route that heads eastwards

Gwern Gof Isaf campsite and Tryfan

to Craig Llugwy and down to a checkpoint at the outlet of the **Ffynnon Llugwy Reservoir** *(water source)*. From here the tarmac reservoir approach road declines to the **A5 at 687603 (O)**.

After crossing the busy road the route continues past Gwern Gof Isaf (campsite) up the desolate cwm of Nant yr Ogof *(water source)*. It climbs out to gain the Glyder Ridge at Llyn Caseg-ffraith, where it joins the old Miners' Path, traversing the grassy saddle between Glyder Fach and Foel Goch before descending bouldery slopes past **control G at 668578** towards the inn at Pen-y-Gwryd. The cascading stream, met on the descent, is a *water source* with numerous pools to cool the feet. The path should be abandoned at the wall-crossing, and a bee-line made westwards for Llyn Cwmffynon. At the north-west side of the lake, a route that has descended from Glyder Fawr takes you down between the rocks to **Pen y Pass Y.H. (P)**, which lies in a barren rocky gorge, the Pass of Llanberis.

From the back right of the cafe car park, follow the heavily engineered Pig Track, which climbs above the Pass of Llanberis before swinging left to Bwlch Goch at the foot of Crib Goch and overlooking lake-filled Cwm Dyli.

The path now veers right traversing the scabby lower slopes of Crib Goch and Carnedd Ugain before coming upon another lake, this time the blue-green Glaslyn. Here the route climbs fri-able water-eroded slopes in zigzags *(water source)* past **con-tol M (GR 614548)** at the junction with the Miners Track to the obelisk at Bwlch Glas. Here the route is joined by the tourist trail from Llanberis, which includes those cute little trains.

While the masses will be heading left for Yr Wyddfa the Welsh 1000s turns its attentions on **Carnedd Ugain (U)** and heads north-eastwards to its summit.

Steps are then retraced to the col before that final climb along the left side of the railway track to **Yr Wyddfa (W)**.

Sporting History of the Welsh 1000 Metres Race

The 1971 inaugural Welsh 1000 Metres Peak Race had nineteen entrants. The fell runners' class was won by Dennis Weir in 3 hours 47 minutes, two minutes outside Ted Norrish's unofficial 1970 record. In the following year, Joss Naylor won in 3 hours 37 minutes, which was to be his best time. Joss was to win the race for five consecutive years. Mike Short broke Naylor's record by forty-five seconds in 1978

In 1979 Access problems required the course to be re-routed. Mike Short won the new race and was to dominate the event into the eighties (five consecutive victories). Since then the race has been won four times by Colin Donnelly who in 1992 set a new the record 3 hours 37:56 minutes

The womens' record was set in 1991 by Carolyn Hunter Davies in a time of 4 hr 30:53.

There are currently four classes in the race:-

A	Fell Runners (minimum age 18)
B	Mountaineers (wearing boots and carrying/ wearing specified items of equipment – minimum age 17)
C	As B but starting from Ogwen (minimum age 15)
D	As B but for service teams (minimum age 18)

There are prizes for men, women, veterans (over 40) and super-veterans (Over 50) and for declared teams.

The race has been re-named "The Snowdonia Summits Marathon" and is organised jointly by the Gorphwysfa Mountaineering Club and the Army in Wales. It is always held

on the first Saturday in June.One Thousand Metres Race (run
1st Saturday in June)

Entry forms are available from Andrew Middleton, 31 Cherry
Tree Avenue, Kirby Muxloe, Leicestershire LE3 3HP

or for services entries (police, army etc):

The Commandant, Capel Curig Training Camp, Gwynedd

The Paddy Buckley Round

by Ronald Turnbull

Ronald's Round

The ridges of Y Garn and Trum y Ddysgl are nice ... but not at midnight. They're still less nice at midnight in mist. At the top of a long gentle grass ridge, everything just stops. There's a sort of path down on the right, but everything gets steeper and steeper, with more and more rocks. The torch shows only a small sphere of grey glare, but there's a feeling of great emptiness all around.

So there I was, crouching to shine my torch onto the vertical boulders to try and tell which ones had been walked on, and ignoring the black hole beyond that could have been six feet of drop, but could equally have been six hundred.

Then at the col the wind blew a brief hole in the cloud, so that I saw unlikely vertical shapes against the sky – which were where I was supposed to go – and distant orange blobs of civilisation – which were where, if I had any sense, I'd already be.

Paddy Buckley's round of forty-seven Snowdonian summits isn't a place for the sensible. Sixty miles horizontal, and 29,000 feet uphill, and involving a certain amount of heather, rock, bog and bracken is just that little bit more than a human being can hope to manage within twenty-four hours. That's the fun of it, of course.

And fun it was, to start with, as I jogged across the footbridge at Plas y Brenin, with Plas y Brenin's canoeists splashing about in the water below. A quick glance to the right showed a lake with a lot of pretty white waves on, which means, if my nautical forebear is to be believed, that we're looking at Force Five here. Beyond the pretty white waves is a brief glimpse of Snowdon. I can't help noticing that the bottom part of Snowdon is quite a long way away and the top part of Snowdon's in cloud.

No time for that. I'm in a nicely scented afternoon forest, but they say that smells and memory occupy the same bit of

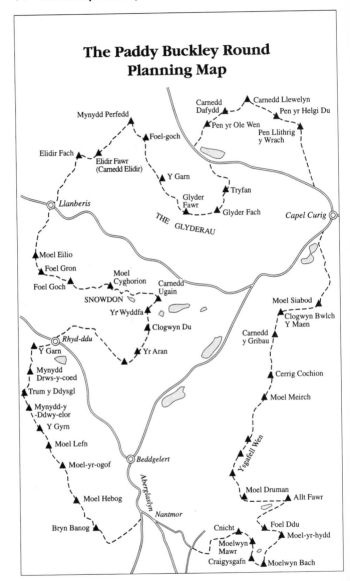

The Paddy Buckley Round
Planning Map

brain and memory's working at high speed here. This is because of the OS Outdoor Leisure map, which has these first three miles printed on the back. The map is inconveniently large. However, the business of refolding it inside out in Force Five will soon reduce it to small manageable-sized pieces scattered all over Snowdonia. So this first three miles is being done on memory and concentration and by looking for footprints in the pine needles.

But soon enough I'm on the open slopes, with the way ahead spread grassy green under the sun, and the only complication is in remembering which of the minor bumps along the fence count towards the forty-seven: to which the answer is 'all of them'. And the ground though low is interesting, and interestingly different from the rest of the Round. Small rocks hold in their hollows sparkling pools or else vicious bits of black bog. A whimsical glacier has sharpened Moel Meirch into a black pencil-point. The path passes by it, but machete-work through the heather bush is rewarded by a ten-second scramble to its rough summit.

But tumbling down the rough grass to the quarries I'm 25 minutes ahead, which is bad: 25 minutes ahead is too fast by far. And mist is wafting across the grey surface of the Llyn Conglog, which is worse – for I've been romantic, or you could call it lazy, and not explored any of this in advance.

John's at the quarries with friendly words and powdered long-distance food. John by car and short walk from Tanygrisiau has reached here a mere ten minutes quicker than me, and this makes me feel briefly to be a real hillrunner. And thus I continue to feel as I scamper the wonderful terraced path across the steeps of Moelwyn Mawr, the path made by miners for the comfort of runners across the rocks and screes, the path with the wild view straight down onto mist.

Alas, it's little use being a hillrunner if you're running the wrong hill. I take an incorrect traverse path from Bwlch Stwlan, and find myself in some particularly inconclusive mist. At the top there's no cairn, but there's only one Moelwyn Bach so I walk the four corners of the plateau and go back down into the inconclusive mist. Various warning signs about deep dangerous holes are ones that warned me on the way up, and I'm pretty sure I'm on the right way back to that Bwlch but

Moelwyn Bach showing the little path that the author missed in the hill fog

better just check the map...

The map shows an isolated contour ring, 300 yds south-east of the summit of Moelwyn Bach. So it's a case of Moelwyn Back we go, to the puddled plateau, and head north-west, and sure enough the ground rises again to somewhere that does have a cairn on it. And right beside that cairn, the quite clear path I should have come up on.

If I knew any blistering Welsh curses I'd be cursing them now. The mist is thick and black, with rain in it, and Moelwyn Mawr's more-or-less OK but there's a long tricky bit across the plateau and a direct route up the south face of Cnicht that no-one in their senses would ever take but only people on the Buckley Round.

I'm just wondering when the south face's going to start getting really steep and nasty when it rolls over like a friendly dog and I'm standing on the ridge path. So what if the ridge is uphill to the right, I know the summit's to the left; and then there's a long gentle runoff, and a rocky craggy place with woods dripping quietly under the bottom edges of the cloud.

After that it's off through some very deep bracken onto a range called the Southern Nantlle, or Eifionydd, or various other things depending on who's doing the calling. That very deep bracken, and a heathery little thing called Y Gyrn (Y

Grymace might be more appropriate), and that too fast start, and doing three Moelwyns where the schedule only said two: these were the various reasons why I ended getting benighted on Y Garn.

Not that that wasn't fun, too. But not the high-intensity 47-in-a-day sort of fun. More disembodied, midnight sort of fun: the Cloud-of-Unknowing sort of fun enjoyed by medieval mountain hermits for whom there's no true virtue in believing the compass reading unless that compass reading's plain impossible.

It was a sort of fun I didn't particularly want a whole lot more of over the rock ridges of Snowdon. So I stopped in the car park, and slept in the parked car till dawn...

Even at dawn, the Snowdon range didn't look attractive. Damp crags had their tops in grey cloud, their feet in brown grass and greenish-brown bog. But having come all the way to Snowdonia, Snowdon is what you have to do. And who knows: the invisible bits up inside the cloud might not be quite so bad as they look.

This turns out to be the case. A grassy edge leads up between two voids of grey air onto Yr Aran. In the col beyond, a silvery pool offers refreshment to the eye and water to the plastic bottle. Clogwyn Du is at its best when the wind blows streamers of mist between the wet little pinnacles. The top of Snowdon is like a seedy theatre at the grey breakfast-time of the morning after, its splendid decoration worn and chipped at the corners, its crowds departed leaving only their empty bottles and crisp wrappers trapped in the cracks of the furniture.

But then on Moel Cynghorion the clouds, which must be connected to a creaky pulley mechanism in the wings, reluctantly rise. The big spotlight in the sky switches on, lakes sparkle like tinsel in windy sunshine, and the wet crags gleam splendidly. It's landscape carved with an axe, this western end of Snowdon. Grass rises towards the sky, turns to give a narrow edge for running along, and then stops abruptly in a sheer drop of hundreds of feet. The scene displays itself briefly, the curtain drops for half-time; but alas, something jams in the pulley system and the second act never happens.

Llanberis is a town built on slate and of slate, living by slate and possibly even eating slate and watching slate on TV. Rain bounces off the car park with real malevolence as I tuck into a nice tin of creamed rice. Beyond the hedge the surface of the lake lies rain-pocked and grey – slaty grey.

A path winds between high walls into the slate-workings, to look back on Llanberis from directly above. Rare plants grow in the crevices of the workings – downy thistles strangely grey in colour. Elidir Fach is a very ordinary hilltop; however it does have real grass growing out of it.

Elidir Fawr is not ordinary, but a fine rocky ridge, even if it does look down on that strangely circular little reservoir with its tarred access road. And man's puny attempts at mountain demolition are finally forgotten along the Glyders. For here the landscape has been demolished by glaciers; glaciers that have gouged great hollows into the northern slopes and left their rubble all along the Round's second Foel Goch, its second Y Garn.

Glyder Fawr's another of those places you don't really get the point of until you visit it in mist. All those little rocky bits sticking out of the boulder field: what are they actually for, and why so many? They stand there as a lesson in shape awareness. You never appreciate a sculpture until you prowl round it in mist, wondering if it's a totally new one or the one you saw before from the other direction. The one that's actually the summit is the second most north-westerly one, and it has a summit cairn, honest it does, on a little platform half way down and round the back where you only see it once you've walked past it convinced that one of the others must be higher.

Glyder Fach is more straightforward. Castell y Gwynt's a jammed logpile, except the logs are stones, and the Cantilever's a seesaw that if it ever swung would shake your bones right out of their sockets. Glyder Fach's an adventure playground for grownups, and when you fall among these boulders there's no mother coming with iodine for your grazed knees. What's coming for you is the Ogwen Valley Rescue Team with their inflatable splint and their stretcher. They won't say 'it'll only hurt for a moment', they won't say anything at all, but they'll silently note down in their notebook that you carried no whistle or survival bag, and that the shoes you were wearing were running shoes.

A nearby spiky place is the top of Bristly Ridge. Really I should be going down Bristly Ridge; but though the 24 hours is an abandoned hope, there's a more pressing cut-off time

ahead. Just six more hours to the dusk of the second night, and
five Carnedds still to do, and before the five Carnedds, Tryfan.

Tryfan is wet, and also rather windy. The few people about
on Tryfan are clinging to its sides like barnacles on a sea
washed rock. It's an awkward clamber up Tryfan's streaming
boulders in clothes stiffened by the weight of absorbed rainwater, and an even more awkward clamber down. Hillrunners –
real hillrunners – have descended Tryfan to the lakeside in
seven minutes dead, or, even harder to credit, in seven minutes
still alive. I take roughly seven times those seven minutes, and
over the jagged lid of another tin of rice, look to something
more straightforward: a simple pull up Pen yr Ole Wen.

Forward – and upward. Except that the top half of it's hidden by the roof of the car. This final climb onto the Carneddau
is two thousand two hundred feet in under a mile. It says 'what
are you, a man or a mouse? Me, I'm a mountain.'

Higher up, it's scree, and optimistic pressing upward
through little gullies between the crags. And now there's real
wind, and quite a lot of it: so that I stop thinking 'a tin of rice
inside and five hours till dark, I'll finish it anyway,' start thinking about the clifftop of the Ysgolion Duon and whether to get
blown over it. Certainly the Ysgolion Duon lie north of my
route while the wind is from the south. And the wind is of the

Pen yr Helgi-du and Pen Llithrig y Wrach from Carnedd Llewelyn

blow-me-down variety, bringing me to a bent halt on the stony ridges of David's Carnedd.

Now I haven't been able to track down a Patron Saint of hill-runners, but undoubtedly there must be one. Whoever it was had a rare bit of fun that afternoon on receiving my unspoken prayer: 'just some ordinary rain and mist, I'm used to that stuff, but how about a break from this wind tunnel bit?'

The wind dropped, became a mere nothing, allowed me even to crouch behind the cairn of Llewelyn's Carnedd and turn the beastly map inside out. And the mist descended: a good thick 'now how's your map-and-compass work' sort of mist. And it rained. It rained a real '... with your map turned to papier mache' sort of rain. It ran in streams down the rocks and up the sleeves of my waterproofs, turned path to instant mud.

Maybe some lesser saint was having a good laugh, but I was having fun too. Compass work I can do, and hillrunning clothes are meant to be soaking wet. And up to Pen yr Helgi Du is one final bit of lovely ridge, rocks and a winding path and two big drops.

And so to the final hill, and down long heather, and out of the simplicity of a compass bearing and a few yards of wet hill to the real world. The real world turned out to be a wide empty place, very flat, with a bit of hillside in the distance and no sign of any of the features that look so significant on the OL map such as the Llugwy valley, or the A5(T). Instead there was a whole lot of waist-high heather.

After a brief but intimate encounter with the heather I found the ancient bridleway, and even the A5(T), and trotted down the road to Plas y Brenin.

At the Plas they were skiing: skiing in the dark on a soaking wet dry ski slope. Some people's idea of sport, strange isn't it?

John and his car, having been there faithfully through two days and a night, now weren't. I was soaking wet, with three Mars bars, £20 and a phone card. The £20 would buy Bed & Breakfast and the Bed at least would be dry, though what to wear to eat the Breakfast in was going to be a problem. But the first thing was to eat the Mars bars. By which time John and his car were there after all. I climbed into some dry clothes and we started driving back towards Scotland.

Four Day Backpack of the Buckley Round

For fellrunners, the big day out in Wales is the Buckley Round. For walkers, the round is the big day out – then the other big day out – and then the third, and the fourth big days out.

Taken as a backpack trip over four days, the Buckley Round is big horizontally – 62 miles. It's big vertically – Snowdon's just an incident in the early hours of Day 4. Most of all, it's a big experience of intensive Snowdonia. All of the high and sharp ridges are walked with the exception of Crib Goch – but you've probably already done Crib Goch. Eight mountain lakes are visited, and two of the nicest of them are slept beside. Sudden edges are looked over, waterfalls are strolled beside, and beneath the shining slates of Llanberis chips are eaten.

Be reassured: you won't have completely used up Snowdonia when you're through. The northern Carneddau are not visited, there's still Y Lliwedd on the Snowdon Horseshoe, and, yes, one or two tops at the western end of Nantlle.

DAY 1: Carneddau, Moel Siabod
Ogwen to Llynnau Diwaunedd
14 miles (23km) 6500 ft (2000m)

The Carneddau are high and stony. The drops over the Ysgolion Duon are quite exciting, until you get to the really exciting ridge to Pen yr Helgi Du: here the drops are on both sides at once. Take afternoon tea at Capel Curig before climbing through the woods onto Moel Siabod.

Two thousand two hundred feet up **Pen yr Ole Wen** is just a matter of getting on with it. Cross the A5 bridge to a signed path up the south ridge. The way starts up a rock crack slightly left. For the first few hundred feet the path is very steep, and has been reconstructed by the path-reconstruction people. Above that it's loose scree and boulders, while remaining very steep. Towards the top it traverses right into the bottom of a well-worn rocky groove. The rocky groove is – need it be said? – very steep. It's a cruel place, where much effort is rewarded only with splendid views of places you've just been driving along.

It's worth it when you get up. Broad stony cragtops lead over the next five miles, with not very much uphill at all, and lots of cragtops to peer over. From the shelter cairn at the top

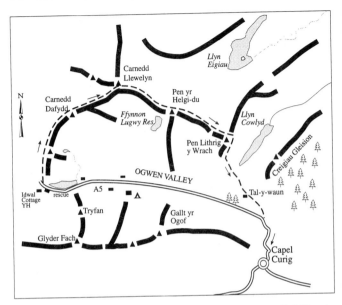

of the steep ascent, enjoy the flatness as you stroll 300 yds north-east to Pen yr Ole Wen's actual summit.

Now a broad stony ridge leads round the head of an eastern cwm to a huge bronze-age cairn (which isn't the top of **Carnedd Dafydd**), and to a slightly smaller contemporary cairn (which is). Continue eastward along the top of the Ysgolion Duon – in wild weather the path slightly down right of the clifftop edge may be preferred. But return to the crest at the point where it dips and turns south-east. Here, just over the northern edge, a sharpish rocky ridge springs out. This leads onto the broad shoulder of **Carnedd Llewelyn**.

Llewelyn itself is a wide flat-topped heap of stones. Long green valleys slide out quietly in various directions, like serpents leaving the ruins of an ancient temple.

The first cairn is a large shelter. Fifty yards north is the actual summit cairn, another bronze age job. Return to the southern cairn, and now be careful to take path south for 100m before turning SE down scree zigzag. This leads onto a gently-descending grass ridge. Do not relax too much. Sharpness and rockiness increase considerably on the approach to the col, with some simple down-scrambling to be done.

Through the col itself and onward towards **Pen yr Helgi Du**, the ridge is fine and narrow. Do not be misled by traverse paths on the right, which head off unhelpfully down the south ridge; take the crest direct. After wrestling with the rocks you emerge onto the peaceful green place that's Helgi's summit, and this slopes down in gentle ridge to a low pass. It's the Bwlch y Tri Marchog: an ancient through route from the heart of Snowdonia to the sea.

Now the credit balance you built up on Pen yr Ole Wen is used up. It's a stiff 600 ft climb onto **Pen Llithrig y Wrach**. The southward descent is steep, on heather. You think it's pretty deep heather till you get to the bottom, where the heather-tips practically tickle your chin. A fence in from the right guides towards the junction of bridleways at 717609 where leats join. Get lost here and you're in deep trouble – deep heather trouble. The fence meets the leat running in from the west at a footbridge; cross and turn left for 200 yds to the leat junction. Now another footbridge crosses the leat in from the east.

The bridleway follows fence and wall as it wanders off left of the leat, rejoining it after 300yds to cross at a third footbridge. Clear at first as it heads south, the bridleway becomes nothing but a bit of field with no rushes growing out. After a ladder stile at the field corner, turn right down the edge of the new field to a track running across left. This leads to Tal y Waun. Pass above the buildings, where a solitary waymark indicates the faint path-line that slants down to reach the A5 at Bron Heulog.

Walk down the road to Capel Curig – there's a sketchy pavement here and there – and turn right. At this corner is a handy cafe: there's a Youth Hostel, and a choice of hotels, a mile away eastward. Or there's a 2000-foot climb up Siabod dead ahead.

Just past the Activity Centre at **Plas-y-Brenin**, a footpath sign points down left. Look to your right as you cross the footbridge over the Llynnau Mymbyr – and what you get depends on the weather. It could be a striking view into the heart of Snowdon's eastern cwm; or it could be grey cloud, whitecaps and a faceful of spray off the lake.

A nice sheltered path leads up through the woods. Here, if your overnight gear's old and disreputable enough not to get

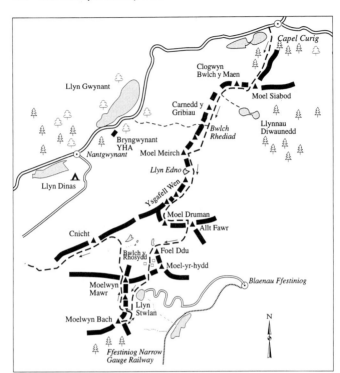

pinched, you hid it as you drove in to Ogwen. At the horizontal track turn right for a few yards, then up the west bank of a stream, to emerge from the trees at a stile.

The going is grassy to **Moel Siabod's** misty trig. The summit pretends to be a rocky place, but down the back it's smooth grass and a fence. Stay with the fence over Clogwyn Bwlch-y-main – on this outing, the smallest hills have the biggest names, but this one really is rocky. Enjoy the brief evening scramble, then turn left at the col and descend 500 steep feet to where two sparkling lakes lie under the long shadow of Carnedd y Gribau.

The twin lakes of Llynnau Diwaunedd are well-sheltered. However, if the weather should be howling out the need for a valley campsite, a forest track leads from the foot of the lake or

Moel Siabod rising from the shores of Llynnau Diwaunydd

lakes down to Blaenau Dolwyddelan.

DAY 2: Moelwyns & Cnicht
Llynnau Diwaunedd to Aberglaslyn
17 miles (27km) 6000 ft (1800m)

Snowdonia north of the A498 is big simple shapes carved by
glaciers. This southern country is different – different from the
North and not even the same as itself, so that at one minute
you're on the ridge and the next it's 50m away. The rock is
close to the surface and in its hollows it holds evil little bogs or
perfect pools. The first pool's held on high as in a cup at the
very summit of **Carnedd y Gribau**.

   If there's any morning sun, it'll be sparkling off the lake
below you. It's a stiff pull back onto the ridge north of Carnedd
y Gribau to start the low but lumpy day. Between the rocks and
the bogs, it's pleasantly grassy. But you can't altogether avoid
the bogs, nor the rocks either, so that occasionally you find
yourself knee-deep in the brown, or dropping over a sudden
small scramble. The sketchy path follows the remains of the old
fence, the one marked on the OL map, to cross Cerrig Cochion.

The old quarries which stretch between Bwlch y Rhosydd and Bwlch Cwmorthin

The fence remnant and path together avoid Moel Meirch, and off the path it's heathery. But **Moel Meirch** is one of the forty-seven, and surprises you with a very small mountain that's rock right to the top. So leave the fence at its bend, slant up across the rock face of Meirch's left-hand knoll to the small col beside its right-hand, summit knoll. On the final spike a single person can balance gingerly – certainly no room for the trig point marked on that OL map.

Return to the nearest point on the path, and let it lead you round the gravelly east end of Llyn Edno and over the very small humps of **Ysgafell Wen**, Moel Llynnau'r-cwn (669m), the unnamed summit (672m) and **Moel Druman**. Few of the forty-seven will be this easy.

A brand new electric fence guides to the col 200m short of the summit of **Allt Fawr**. Here you glance down towards the urban dereliction of Blaenau Ffestiniog, thank the weather gods for any thick mist that prevents your actually having to see the place, then backtrack along the southern shore of Llyn Conglog. Cross the outflow and continue straight ahead, ascending slightly, then dropping down a long shapeless ridge with steep slopes on the left and a small reservoir (Llyn

Cwm-corsiog) ahead. Pass left of the reservoir, to pick up the old track at the corner of its dam.

At the disused quarries GR 665462, quarrymen's cottages are crumbling elegantly back into the piles of slate they were made from. Here an incline leads south-east onto a flattish boggy area. Cross it eastwards onto **Foel Ddu**. It's short walk south then up to Moel-yr-hydd.

Now descend west to the corner of a huge quarry hole, and pick up the path southwards (the lower of the two on the map). It's not yet time to climb Moelwyn Mawr, and this track traverses round its flank to Bwlch Stwlan, the col between it and Moelwyn Bach. This flank of Moelwyn Mawr is steep and broken but the path, built in stone terraces by helpful miners, is a treat no matter how unwieldy the sack. You look down across man-made levels and slate-tippings to the reservoir of Stwlan. Unfortunately the slate-workings have recently been reactivated, so we'll have to wait another half-century before they again become aged and interesting dereliction.

From Bwlch Stwlan, go up briefly to the foot of **Moelwyn Bach's** rock snout. Now, round left, a path slants up across scree to approach the summit from due east. Take time, if necessary, to find this path: all other ways are appalling.

Back on the Bwlch, take the narrow rocky ridge of Craigysgafn to **Moelwyn Mawr**. After all the rough ground,

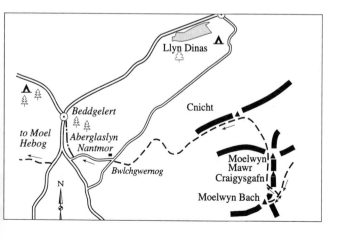

Moelwyn Mawr's grassy dome is a place to lie down on and gaze back, across all the rocks and pools, to Moel Siabod; or to look anxiously forward to Snowdon.

Descend northwards and pass right of Llyn Croesor to revisit those crumbling quarry buildings on their plateau of loose slates. Pick up the path northwards to the end of Cnicht's east ridge at GR 657477. Meanwhile pity the poor fellrunners who to save a couple of minutes are taking Cnicht's south face direct.

A bit of a Cnife-edge is **Cnicht**, with a serrated grey edge. It's a popular, well sat-on place, with cosy nooks to linger in and watch the sun go down across Tremadog Bay. The descent is long but gentle. You scramble down slightly left on a well-worn path, then take the grassy crest. At the 400m contour, a rocky rise is avoided on the right. Now waymarks start to appear, pointing to a grass track parallel to the crest but 100 yds down on the right. More waymarks at GR 628451 indicate the right turn onto the 'road used as public path'. It's a stony track, part of the Roman road Sarn Helen – though I wouldn't want to walk it myself in hobnailed sandals. The track turns sharp right to slant down through trees to tarmac at Bwlchgwernog. It's a shame to come off the hill onto the road? Well, this narrow one to **Aberglaslyn** is poor in traffic, but contrariwise rich in hill; its gradients will tax your end-of-day ankles.

Nantmor's accommodation is limited: this gives you a chance to explore northwards towards Beddgelert. And if your bed should be Beddgelert, the exploring northwards is a treat. From the back corner of the car park, an old railway line leads through three tunnels. One of the tunnels is long enough to require some groping in the dark, or, less excitingly, a torch.

It may be dark in the tunnels, but you'll be hoping for daylight outside. For what's outside is all the rainwater off the southern side of Snowdon – and that's a lot of rainwater – running through a valley that's 50m wide. The craggy side-walls, the overhanging trees, the perched road and even you on your railway embankment: all seem uncomfortably squeezed and ready to fall into the river and get swept away.

After a mile, cross the footbridge to enter **Beddgelert** along the river's west bank. Beddgelert is the burying place of Prince

Llewelyn's dog. The tomb of this mythic hillrunning animal is on the left just before the village.

DAY 3: Eifionydd
Aberglaslyn to col north of Yr Aran
13 miles (21km) 7100 ft (2100m) or
to Llyn Ffynnon-y-gwas 16 miles (26km) 9300 ft (2800m)

This is the group with only one easy hill. The single contour-ring of Mynydd-y-Ddwy-elor takes less time to walk over than to say. But Hebog is cruel and steep: before it, Bryn Banog is just as steep and covered with bracken. Moel Ogof and Moel Lefn have crags to find your way around, or to fall over, while Y Gryn is some stuff that slopped out of the skip when they were taking the rubbish away to dump it on the Rhinogs. (Those of us who think the Rhinogs are wonderful will enjoy Y Gryn and wish there was more of it). But the end repays all. Mynydd Drws-y-coed is the most exciting high ridge of the Round; it makes you not mind at all missing out Crib Goch.

The longer option lets you continue to get Snowdon's South Ridge all beautiful and lonely in the evening light. But the South Ridge and Snowdon are just as beautiful – and just as lonely – in the clear light of dawn, and the third day is when you're at your worst. So start luxuriously late from the B&B and keep it short.

Cross the Afon Glaslyn and turn south on the A498 for 200 yds. Just above the driveway of **Aberglaslyn Hall**, a path slants uphill. Cross a stream, and zigzag up through woods just beyond it onto bracken-clad fields. The route, not visible on the ground, goes uphill SW to pass left of ruined farm buildings. Continue by a small stream to stile at GR 577453. This leads onto open hill below Bryn Banog (519m spot height).

That open hill is, as already mentioned, steep. Go straight up onto Bryn Banog, where a pleasant horizontal ridge leads northwards. Here you can forget the steep climb behind in the contemplation of the steep and rather rocky face of **Moel Hebog** ahead. To reach it, turn west at the ridge end to cross a boggy and confusing col. The face of Moel Hebog goes surprisingly easily up the green hollow of a small stream.

Hebog was the hard work: ahead lie two smaller hills that are rocky and rewarding. Descend from Hebog NW; the slope

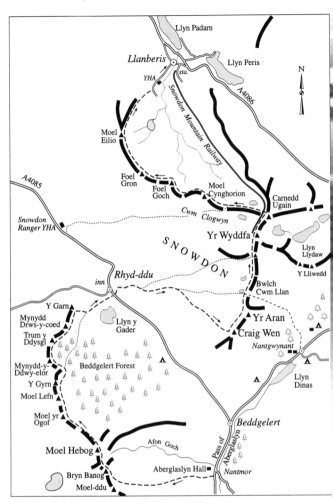

is steep but grassy, and there's a comfortable bit of path. From the col follow the fence, if you dare, into a remarkable little chasm. There's no need to worry: if dragons do lurk here, they can only be very small ones as there's not much room. Rocky ground leads on to **Moel yr Ogof**. The brief descent to the col beyond may need a compass bearing in mist, as there's no clear ridge-line or path.

A direct northward descent off **Moel Lefn** would lead to crags. Take time to find the small path that winds down left-ward to rejoin the crest for the flatter section around 450m altitude. As the ridge prepares to steepen again, drop right to the forest corner.

The 450m bump just ahead is Y Gyrn. A path circumvents it to the west, but it's one of the forty-seven. Though it may not look much from here, from the valley below it's a fine spike on the horizon that you'd be sorry to have missed. A stone wall leads up through the deep heather: it's easiest just to right of the wall. Keep to rock tops rather than undergrowth where possible. It's grass again once you get to Bwlch-y-Ddwy-elor.

The final ridges are exposed enough that, in really high wind with a really large sack, it's wiser to avoid them. In which case take, with bitter regrets, the bridleway north-west from Bwlch-y-Ddwy-elor. A stile at col leads into forest.

Follow the fence to the minor hump of Mynydd-y-Ddwy-elor (466m), then stroll the long gentle grass ridge above. It's got a shock at the top. The grass stops – just like that – and you're peering down into the deep hole of the Nantlle valley. For here the glacier has carried out one of its terribly simple effects, chopping off half the mountain and carrying it away into the Irish Sea.

Across the deep hole, the sunny cliffs of Craig y Bera smile back at you. Just a couple of wing beats away for a Nantlle raven, they're 2000 feet down and up again on vertical grass both ways and out of reach of this particular long-distance expedition.

It takes a moment to adjust to the way everything's suddenly gone vertical, and to discover that if you head off over the brink eastward you don't slide screaming into the northern corries but find, a few metres down the curve of oblivion, a sharp ridge springing out of the side of the mountain. There's a small path, and no actual rock climbing, and mostly you're a few feet down on the southern side of the crest. That's the side that isn't altogether vertical.

You won't want to be on this next col when it's windy. On a calm day, though, it's a place of rare perfection: a strip of narrow grass between green chasms, and overlooked by a sheer corner of **Mynydd Drws-y-coed**.

Mynydd Drws-y-coed has no cairn – a cairn might finally overbalance the mountain and send it toppling into the Nantlle valley. The nervous path stays a few feet below the highest point, on the southern slope. More rock-and-grass ridge-work leads on eastwards, with a little downhill scrambling at one point.

Y Garn is wider. Y Garn has room to move around and examine the huge and ancient cairns, but it's still the end of everything. Peer over the stone wall and you're suddenly looking down at 500 ft (150m) of nothing with Rhyd Ddu at the bottom. Only the narrow neck of land behind you connects Y Garn to anything at all; do the cairns contain the bones of thousands who have arrived here and never found any way off?

Off is in fact possible. Grass slopes lead south-west then south, keeping to the right of considerable craggy bits. At the bottom, a bridleway marked with white paint marks leads NE to a corner of the B4418.

Join the road (GR 566526) and immediately leave it at a track on the right. A waymarked footpath follows the track then field edges to a footbridge. A flagged path over fields leads to the **Rhyd Ddu** car park at the bottom of Snowdon. As well as the sparkling Llyn y Gader to look at Snowdon over, Rhyd Ddu has a useful pub.

Take the track 100 m north of the car park, keeping straight ahead when the popular Rhyd Ddu Path up Snowdon turns left after a mile. Once over the stream at 350m altitude, strike south-east across open moor. A fence leads up to the col north of **Craig Wen**, with that 608m summit a few minutes away south-west.

A fine grass ridge leads onto **Yr Aran**. The descent of Yr Aran is steep, and will give trouble even if you've not got benighted. The new fence contours below the summit on the southern side, but you soon rejoin it as you descend the north-east ridge, to meet a stone wall. Contour west for 200 yds, just above the wall, to reach the northern spur of the mountain. Turn downhill, alongside the wall, to the col with its small pool.

This high-perched tarn looks out through the gap of the Nantlle valley to the sea. In that sea you should see reflected

Mynydd Drws-y-coed from Y Garn

the sunset of a long and golden day. But in wilder weather, the tarn half a mile north will be more sheltered. In worse weather than that, you can descend eastward on a path that starts steep and loose, but becomes a grass tramway along the Cwm Llan. Nantgwynant has B&Bs and a Youth Hostel.

DAY 4: Snowdon and The Glyders
Col north of Yr Aran to Ogwen
19 miles (30km) 9200 ft (2800m)

Start early, and you can cross the entire Snowdon massif without meeting a soul. You should start early, on this last and longest day; and since you're starting from camp, you should manage to do so. On the long runoff towards Moel Eilio you could be persuaded you're on a mountain range that's not all that popular.

The Glyders you've probably been on before. But have you been on the Glyders in mist and rain... in heat when the very stones sizzle and vibrate... in snow, in wind that shrieks around the rock-turrets? The Glyders are good, and good in different ways, in every different sort of weather.

The day starts with the fine sharpness of Snowdon's South Ridge. The path runs along cosily, just to the right of the crest, high above **Cwm Llan**. Sunrise blazes behind the jagged crest of Y Lliwedd, and at 8:00 am there's no need to queue for the

The Snowdon Train with Moel Cynghorion and Moel Eilio behind.

privilege of sitting on Snowdon's summit trig. In two or three hours this'll become a busy and cheerful place, with ice creams and a dear little toy train. But when dawn shadows fill the valleys of mankind, **Snowdon** Summit returns to a time when eagles really did nest in Eryri.

Scamper down the large built path to the obelisk at the top of the Pig Track (993m spot height), and up well-trodden path to **Carnedd Ugain** – the quickest trig-to-trig in Wales. Drop west to cross stone-fields, the wide Llanberis Path and the railway, to the wide Snowdon Ranger Path. Descend its zig-zags, or the crest on the right, to the col above Llyn Ffynnon-y-gwas. As an alternative campsite, this lake shortens the final day by three miles and 2,000 ft.

Small paths wander onward over **Moel Cynghorion**. Crags are all around but you're on the gentlest of grass, with a fence alongside to guide you. It's a place to linger on a warm forenoon and watch the sparkling of the waters in Cwm Clogwyn. Only the cairn of Foel Gron, teetering on the brink of a terrific crag, gives a brief moment of non-tranquillity.

Moel Eilio, perched on the end of the range, is a softer sort of mountain. Look back along the ridge to Snowdon, marvelling at how far you've come, and ignore for now the dark

Glyders laid out for your consideration along the far side of
Nant Peris.

Follow the fence northward, to the fence junction at 650m.
Path and fence lead down the north-east ridge, with handsome
ladder-stiles at every cross-fence. At 250m a stile leads onto a
horizontal cross-track. Turn right for 200 yds. A gate on the left
opens onto the tarred lane past a small campsite and the Youth
Hostel to **Llanberis**. You can carry your lunch all the way over
Snowdon – or you can have chips in Llanberis.

From the back of the main car park (580602), a lakeside
path leads round to the footbridge GR 586602 (the down-
stream bridge, wrongly marked as road bridge on the Outdoor
Leisure map). Cross, and turn right for 200 yds to the end of
the road bridge. Opposite the bridge, a footpath zigzags up
through trees and slate-workings. There's a fine view back
between the tree trunks to the rooftops of Llanberis and the
grey waters of its lake.

Cross a footbridge to turn right onto trackbed below. Follow
this along and up to horizontal track (marked on map as right-
of-way). The man-made landscape of gouged quarry and
Llanberis is almost as good as the rest of the grim Glyders.

Traverse SE along the horizontal track. Some height will
have to be lost before the right of way emerges onto open
slopes above Fron farm. Turn uphill to the right of the quarry
workings to **Elidir Fach**. Cross the wide col south-west to

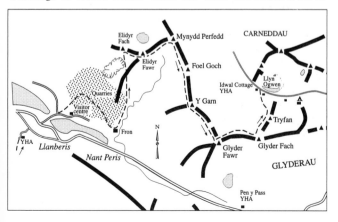

keep right of stone-fields, but get stone-fields anyway on the sharpening crest of **Elidir Fawr**.

The Glyders lie before you. To start with, they're an ordinary bit of nice ridge, with long slopes rising to a crest. There's a rocky scramble along the top if you want it, but a path down on the right as well to cross the col. The path on the right doesn't just avoid the scrambly bits, it avoids **Mynydd Perfedd** as well: leave it and strike up grassy slopes above.

Descend Mynydd Perfedd by the fence to rejoin the path in the next col. But the path is after the three-thousanders, and now it wants to avoid **Foel-goch** as well. So leave it immediately after the col to strike up the scree above on faint zig-zags. For Foel-goch is where it starts to be more than merely another nice ridge-walk to put on the end of the fifty miles of nice ridge-walk you've already done. Foel-goch is more glacier-hacked landscape. Here the northern half of the mountain's been taken away and instead you get a 2500 ft hole with a sparkling river in the bottom. It's an effect seen already on Snowdon's Foel Gron, on Mynydd Drws-y-coed; but if you're tired of the sudden missing mountainside you're tired of life. In which case, the north edge of Foel-goch is an ideally convenient spot to end it all.

Walk the gentle plateau southwards to rejoin that three-thousanding path that doesn't know what it's missed, and let it take you up **Y Garn**, and down the back to the Llyn y Cwn or 'Dog Lake'. From here, the path north is the last easy escape to Ogwen in case night's threatening to fall before you really want it to. For from here, Glyder stops being like anywhere you've been already. From here, it's stones and rocks all the way. The stones are big ones, and arranged into peculiar shapes. And the rocks congeal into crags, to make this fractured plateau an awkward place to get away from.

Stones and rocks make for a long tough pull up the slope east of Llyn y Cwn. The rough scree-path is marked in its upper stage with confusing cairns.

Boulders mostly lie flat on the ground, but on the Glyder plateau they've applied some sort of high-altitude hair gel and are determined to stick up just as high as they possibly can. **Glyder Fawr** has half a dozen of these little rocky surprises.

Splintered boulders, cairns and a path head east across the plateau. The path is not all that visible as it crosses rock-fields,

The summit of Glyder Fawr

but as the ground rises towards the summit of Y Gribin, it traverses the top of the steep slope on the right flank to reach Bwlch-y-Ddwy-Glyder.

Now round right on the southern slope, then up, is the way to avoid the outcrop of **Castell y Gwynt**. Watch out for scratch-marks on the boulders to guide you. Once on the plateau, with the Castell's jammed boulderpile on your left, turn back east. **Glyder Fach's** summit lumps are extremely classy ones but there are only three of them, so you shouldn't get too confused. Well, not unless you're looking for the non-existent trig point the OL Map has playfully placed on the true summit. That summit is a heap of boulders with holes in. If you

Adam and Eve on Tryfan's summit

brought a trained marmot, you could retrieve many valuable compasses and woolly hats from the interior of the pile.

Pass left of the famous Cantilever to the spiky outcrop that's the top of Bristly Ridge and go down eroded scree immediately beyond. (Or else scramble down Bristly Ridge, of course.) Opposite the base of Bristly Ridge paths recombine to traverse left into Bwlch Tryfan.

Cross the col beside the stone wall, to take the first rocks direct, or, more easily, to slant up the left flank by paths and boulder-scrambles. A section of stone wall drops in and out of the small col (GR 663592) behind **Tryfan's** South summit. From this col, the easiest way is again by paths and boulders on the left flank. Once on the crest, a sudden emptiness directly ahead marks the top of the eastern cliffs. Walk round left to the two upright rocks that are Tryfan's summit. Is the proper climax to a backpack such as this, to leap from Adam to Eve while wearing the full long-distance rucksack? I didn't fancy it myself.

Return to the col (663592) before South Top. Descend scree-gully westwards, with paths, and then grass to Llyn Bochlwyd outflow. Go down the rough path to right of the outflow stream, and then a well-built path to **Ogwen**. Is that Snowdonia done now, or will it be necessary to come back?

I think you'll find it necessary to come back.

WALK FACTS

Start/Finish:	Ogwen Cottage GR 648604. Or anywhere else on the circuit, such as the romantic railway stations at Snowdon summit and Tanygrisiau
Distance:	60 mls 100 km
Ascent:	29000 ft 8700 m (Everest exactly)
Terrain:	Grassy rock ridges, stony rock ridges, and rocky ridges. Plus everything in between
Difficulties:	Tricky navigation and route finding, some of it among high crags. An awful lot of uphill. Simple scrambling (easy Grade 1) at various points.
Maps:	1:25000 Outdoor Leisure Snowdonia, plus 2 mls of Landranger 124 (Dolgellau)
Accommodation:	Ogwen (YH only), Capel Curig, Blaenau Ffestiniog, Nantmor, Rhyd Ddu, Llanberis

The Dragon's Back

by Ronald Turnbull

Fifty miles a day, day after day, with the Parachute Regiment carrying the tent: this, we must suppose, is a foretaste of what awaits the dedicated hillrunner in the afterlife.

Enter Wales at the top end; sleep all night, eat large military meals, and run all day, following roughly John Gillham's *'Snowdonia to Gower'* long-distance route. Emerge five days later somewhere near Swansea. There would be the cream of British fell running, as well as eminent guests from abroad. There would be television cameras. There would be a bus to the station afterwards.

There was one thing I didn't ask myself. Does the Dragon's Back Race represent the eventual reward of the well-behaved hillrunner – or of the wicked one?

Competitors eagerly await the start of the race by the walls of Conwy Castle　　　　　　　　　　　　　　　　　Photo: Ian Waddell

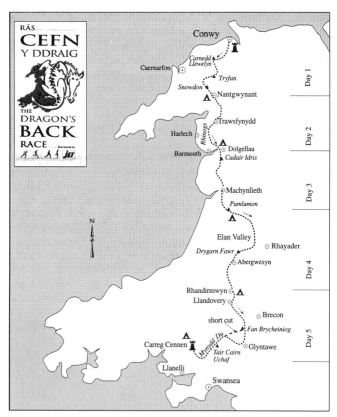

Day 1: The Carneddau, Glyders and Snowdon

In the car park of Conwy Castle, they were interviewing runners for the TV: but not us. We weren't glamorous like the smart and sponsored Americans; nor, so early in the race, quite as ragged and romantic looking as we were soon going to be. The Mayor of Conwy was there in his golden chain. No cannon or whistles for us, for we are after all hillrunners. "All right, off you go then," said the Mayor.

Below the castle walls and through the streets we trotted, with a motorcycle escort and camera van at the front, and also (we realised when the back became us) at the back. We discussed things with the solitary Swede and decided that everyone else had started much too fast for 200 miles. Then we dodged off into a gateway. Our personal route preference is for the pretty way not the quick one, the field paths not the road.

Without so much as a faint gulping sound the wide Welsh landscape swallowed up 57 runners. We climbed Drum alone.

At dawn the hilltops had looked all sunny and bright, and I'd let the Parachute Regiment carry the altimeter. But now the ridge was a misty one. Never mind, navigation's more interesting without altimeters. A pair from Chelmsford found our navigation particularly interesting. We stopped to look at our map: they stopped to look at their map. We stopped to put on our waterproof trousers: they stopped to put on their waterproof trousers. The entrants for this race were supposed to have been vetted for basic hill skills, but the Chelmsford pair had trained on abandoned railway lines, where hill skills are hard to acquire.

The ridge off Carnedd Llewelyn is narrow and exciting, but Glyn had to pause to pour away the rainwater pooling in his lenses. The Chelmsford pair paused too, but they wore no spectacles, and the view wasn't the sort you stop to look at, being mostly mist. Anyway there was only one way to go; so they went. A few minutes later we dropped out of the mist. On the track below there were no runners. The Chelmsford pair had gone onward for Pen yr Helgi Du and points beyond, and plunged into oblivion off the extreme end of the Carneddau.

The track past the reservoir is smooth and level after the stony slopes. Here we could stretch out, and try to look a bit impressive for the Telegraph's photographer. But there came an angry shout from behind. On this fast easy ground Glyn had wrenched his leg. He'd expected injury – it'd be unrealistic to set off for two hundred miles without expecting injury – but he hadn't expected injury so soon.

Still, injury doesn't have much effect on strength uphill, and strength uphill is what we now required. Tryfan and the Glyders lay ahead, and beyond the Glyders, Snowdon. The 9:00am start was convenient for mayors and camera people, but meant that, for us, it was 1:30pm already.

We crossed the A5 onto Tryfan's North Ridge – an irrational route-choice? The camera people lurking in the gully didn't know. They'd lurked on the Heather Terrace only to see all the elite runners head up the North Ridge; then transferred to the North Ridge to see all the midfield runners heading across onto the Terrace. This confirmed what I already had suspected. Glyn and I are elite runners: we're just extremely slow elites. They proceeded to film our elite feet scrabbling up the scree.

The North Ridge has real rock moves. We balanced across the tops of rock climbs, their final pitches rising out of the mist. I, at least, did in distant youth accomplish one or two of those rock climbs, so could be confident that Glyn would be finding this more scary than I was. This is fine psychology. Deal with anxiety by bringing someone you know is going to find it worse.

At the summit, we were fifth last. This wasn't us overtaking, it was people in front getting lost. We lost time, making sure not to climb Bristly Ridge, and then some more, examining the various tops of Glyder First-one, then casting about for the ridge to Glyder Other-one. Casting about on wet splintered boulderfields is no fun.

Four-twenty at Pen y Pass, and it was going to be dark at eight. The weather was horrible but we were fine – there'd been a couple of runners in Bwlch Tryfan who were totally bewildered and we weren't; we'd found both Glyders; and now we had a nice straightforward Pig Track along which to eat our sandwiches.

Runners in proper lightweight gear can enjoy the wind and rain. Even stranger, so can runners like us in washed-out tee-shirts and waterproofs whose breathability is assured by torn seams and various holes. It's a matter of charging into battle rather than sitting in a shellhole being shot at. It's getting sweaty enough actually to welcome rainwater next to the skin. And when you're already leaping around on a high ridge with hardly any clothes on, vigorous gusts of wind just make it more exciting. Since I was last on it, the Pig Track had become a Pig Road, with boulder-steps and flat gravel. An hour and twenty minutes up Snowdon – we were indeed enjoying ourselves. At the top was an orange tent containing Ian Waddell. This man had devised this inspiring route, gathered sponsors, TV coverage and the Parachute regiment. His reward was to spend eleven hours on Snowdon summit with a boulder under his groundsheet. We had to admit that including all the 3000ft peaks on this first day wouldn't have been a good idea after all. Before the race I'd written to Ian pointing out what a classic first day the full 3000s would have made. He'd awarded me the race number of [1] for attitude, but explained he couldn't be bothered putting an orange tent on Yr Elen.

We headed off down the twisting, exhilarating South-west Ridge. But once among the lovely woods and waterfalls of Cwm Llan, on pleasant green track, Glyn wrenched his leg again. He added to the sufferings of the unfortunate limb by insulting it most viciously.

We arrived at 7:02 pm – eighteenth; so while we were lost on the Glyders we must have been overtaking others even more lost. The leading pair of Martin Stone and Helen Diamantides took just under seven hours: now that's fell running. We ate supper, drank eight cups of coffee and juice and finally got the fluid balance right. We then ate another supper and inspected the shower. British military ingenuity was the shower, comprising duckboard, bucket and pulley. The person underneath thought it was great, but we were only going to get dirty again tomorrow.

Day 2: The Moelwyns and Rhinogs

At the start they said, "Anyone want this midfield runner, lost his partner?" Perhaps unwisely, I said yes. In fact Stefan from Frankfurt didn't lose his partner. His partner dumped him after a depressing twelve-hour yesterday. Stefan is 28 and goes in for the Hundred Kilometre, also the Geneva to Basle 'hill' race, which actually takes place on roads and paths. He was certainly very good on the roads and paths, but once up in the grassy rocky valley with the waterfalls and the croaking ravens, he turned out to be wearing unsuitable shoes. Soon enough we were back in the clouds, and the pair behind wanted to know which hill this was. Well, it was Moelwyn Mawr, and since we were going quite slowly anyway with our ill-shod German, we thought we'd show them the way off Moelwyn Bach.

The way we showed them off Moelwyn Bach was a really terrible one, clambering down all the little cliffs. At one point Glyn abseiled a tree root. Our entourage found this even slower than we did. If there was a certain vagueness in their thoughts and movements, there was good reason. This pair spent half the night crossing Snowdon, having previously gone up something else by mistake for Tryfan. At the railway it was a relief to wave good-bye and dash ahead down the track.

It's funny how this always happens. You wave good-bye and dash away down the track, and it turns out to be the wrong track, so you end up coming back up it and waving hello again. The railway alongside makes the same mistake, turning a complete circle and going underneath itself at Dduallt station. My sister's boyfriend worked as a guard on the Ffestiniog railway, and found himself involved in a hi-jacking episode. In the long run, you're best on your own two feet.

The next bit cheered everybody up. It's a man-made surface, which reminded Stefan of his happy Hundred Kilometre. That surface, however, is tilted sharply upwards, and goes among rough heather and rougher boulderfields, and the men who made it are referred to as 'Romans' though probably 17th-century Welsh.

When the Karrimor Mountain Marathon went over my home hills of Galloway, people said: "It's almost as bad the Rhinogs." So I'd been looking forward to these Rhinogs. They didn't let me down. The Roman pavement entered a dramatic defile. Mist blew over, and, though no Welsh bandits were in evidence, they're scarcely needed. The boulder-fields alongside the path will do the same job of breaking your legs for you and leaving your body for the ravens. I urged my party forward with hoarse cries; 2:00pm at the Roman Steps meant darkness on Diffwys.

Quite quickly we were through the pass, and onto the real Rhinog. The real Rhinog is jammed grey gritstone. The boulders show admirable sincerity in their project – to make two two-thousand foot hills into an impenetrable mountain range. Above Rhinog Fawr's small lake, Stefan hoped there wasn't going to be any 'scramblink'. He learned this useful English word on Tryfan, and seemed to understand it quite as well as he wanted to. But the jammed boulders tilted up alarmingly, and Stefan became cragbound. "Nein es geht nicht, es ist gefährlich zu Lebens," he said in his fluent German. "Niemand ist hier gesterben" I reassured him in my broken German.

Nobody dies hereabouts. "Niemand?" "Ist Wahrheit." He clambered up a boulder, and another, and mist closed round to hide the black waters below.

The bigger Rhinog overcome, we tore over the smaller one. My diary records 35 min up and 15 down. These hills are high on rock and romance, but sadly small in all other ways. Beyond was ground of a sort we'd almost forgotten: green and grassy, laid out as ridge rather than piled as heap. We galloped down the pleasant slopes, and were at Diffwys with just time to get off the hill before dark.

Well, that was the idea. Somehow it didn't work in practice. And since I was at the front, it must have been me that read the map wrong and landed us up in several miles of tussocky bog and a forest, though I blamed Stefan for being so slow. Along the bog-trudge poor Stefan got a lot of stick, to which must be added twigs-down-the-neck when it got dark as we were still fighting the Christmas trees. It's just as well he doesn't understand English.

Once on the tarmac Stefan ran away strongly. I tried to keep

Martin Stone refuelling in the big green tent   Photo: Ian Waddell

up for the glory of Scotland, but Glyn really dislikes road running, even when it's not in the dark. At last we got to the big green tents. We certainly got value for money from the event's trifling £10 entry fee. We were on our legs for 13½ hrs today.

Stone and Diamantides took just 8¼ hours. Martin Stone said that he couldn't cope with the long hours we were doing at the back of the field. This was pure politeness: he has run 26 Munros non-stop.

Day 3: Cadair Idris, The Tarrens and Plynlimon

I told registration that we didn't want Stefan any more. They said OK, but five minutes down the road, there he was running along beside us. As it turned out, though, it was us that would be slow on Day Three. We strode up Cadair Idris's Pony Track. At the top was another windy rocky ridge with views of mist-filled emptiness.

Smooth grass that's fairly steep downhill can make you feel like a member of the Parachute Regiment yourself, but Stefan didn't appreciate it, and neither on this occasion did Glyn. First Glyn's shoes had gone, and then that ankle again, and a thigh. And now, most undignified of all, came the collapse of his bumbag. The bumbag, as an out-of-fashion fashion item, had been bought very cheaply. However, unlike Glyn, it had been designed and constructed with city streets in mind.

We took three hours over Cadair Idris and were last but two; but still moving, in which respect we were doing better than many on this unprecedented hill race. They filmed Glyn's collapsed shoes running through a ford.

Painfully we ambled into a place called Abergynolwyn. Trying to be helpful, I asked if the muscular physiotherapist could rendezvous with Glyn's leg damage at the next check-point. They seized on the word 'injury' and radioed it back and forth. We hobbled away onto the Tarrens before they could strap us down to any stretchers. The Tarrens are rounded grassy hills with plantations creeping up the sides, overwhelming the very ridge. What was I doing on these Tarrens? I've got better hills at home in the Southern Uplands.

We trotted down through lots of forest to the checkpoint at Machynlleth. It was 3:15, and there were still fifteen miles to the top of Plynlimon; and just as far to the top of Pumlumon, which is the same hill spelt in proper Welsh. We were last through. Over the next section race organiser Ian Waddell would act as escort and guardian angel. In theory the Guardian

Angel jogs along 50 yds behind, observing but giving no navigational aid. We contemplated going round a corner and putting on a quick sprint – just a joke. Glyn alternated walk and shamble and made quite strong progress, specially once we got off the road. All the same the Guardian Angel got bored, and caught up for a chat. It was fun trying to tempt the Angel into navigational hints. "Now that must be Plynlimon." I indicated a point in the distant south, lying dim and grey across the horizon. Ian went very quiet. I looked at the map. Dammit, that actually was Plynlimon!

It was only encroaching dusk lending distance to the view. This bit, that I'd expected to be a bore, went quite pleasantly. A grass road ran along the high moor, (sometimes we even managed to run along the grass road), while on either side were deep valleys full of green shadow, waterfalls and spruce. Much of the Southern Uplands has less to offer.

But at 6:15pm, at the track end under Plynlimon, Ian told Glyn he must retire. Glyn knew that he could get over Plynlimon by nightfall, and even if he couldn't, he's got lots of experience of not getting over things before nightfall. He also knows that the race organiser's right even when he's wrong. Reluctantly, he climbed into the Landrover.

My own feet were blistered from the road running of the previous evening, but though it made me feel slightly jaded, it didn't matter uphill. Stefan and I strode up Plynlimon in the last of the light. The top of Plynlimon at dusk was two piles of stones, grey mist and a little orange tent. We did proper running down the back of Plynlimon, both for the fun of it and also to get away before the grass path crawled into the darkness and pulled the rushes up over its head. We got in at 8:10 without having to use torches. In other words, we didn't get benighted!

Glyn could go on tomorrow if the Medical Sergeant said OK. This was a fairly transparent device by Ian to avoid having to give the bad news himself – fair enough, good even. I could take my own blisters back to Scotland.

Glyn went under the Medical Sergeant, receiving ice, massage and painkillers. Stefan was having a toe lanced. I offered up my blisters. I had trench foot – how glamorous – just like in World War One. And every other war since the Romans, the

Sergeant pointed out... We all turned in feeling much better for this display of military expertise in the field of chiropody. Maybe armies march on their stomachs, but runners run on our feet.

Day 4: Drygarn Fawr

The blisters came back up again in the night. Another 85 miles of slow jogging on blisters wasn't going to be altogether enjoyable but I decided to start anyway. I joined Glyn in the long queue for the Medical Sergeant. The Medical Sergeant gave Glyn's leg no more than ten miles, but he could start. So we did.

The well-wrapped blister became uncomfortable after the first mile but then didn't get any worse. A long trek along forest tracks led to seven miles of road. This middle bit of Wales isn't very mountainous.

I ran with fellow back-markers Chris and John from Teesside. They were both moderately damaged, but quite enjoying the road, and were well supported by Chris' dad. Their car boot was full of bananas, which they generously handed around at every lay-by.

We turned off at last for some intricate rights of way through farm and woodland. The farmland is interrupted by small raven-haunted crags: pretty countryside, and pretty navigation too. Away from the road, Chris had got separated from his painkillers. "Don't worry," said Glyn: "that nice Medical Sergeant gave me more than I can use." There followed a technical discussion on the merits of various painkillers from which I, as a mere blister-sufferer, was excluded.

The way rose above the vast seas of industrial Birmingham's drinking water, on a stony path, a grassy path, and a high green lane between grown-out hedges. Lovely running country, except that we were walking. I did some running for a couple of miles so as to enjoy a stationary chat with Chris Senior in a lay-by tucked away in a wooded valley where buzzards buzzed around with bits of twig in their claws doing nest repairs.

Chris Senior, like Ian Waddell, is an ex-Para; they give themselves away by referring to any part of the landscape as a feature. He told of the battle-march: ten miles in under two hours with 50lbs on the back. He admitted he could go into the toilet with a map and not come out for an hour. He was a bit annoyed at his supporting role. He didn't like us having all the fun.

Drygarn Fawr was the day's one hill. We worked our way onto it on a path that showed every sign of giving out three miles short of the crucial orange tent. We cut across the moor and Glyn came to a sudden halt. His bad leg wouldn't lift over the tussocks. This could lead to an absurd situation - "please winch us out, my friend can't get his leg over" - but we returned to the path and followed it until it collapsed to its final resting-place in a bit of black bog. By this time we were higher up where the tussocks were correspondingly lower.

Drygarn Fawr was only our second hill out of cloud, and a thoroughly dull one apart from two fine beehive cairns. There's a nice way off, a little stream valley carved out below the level of the moor. It's not the quickest way - indeed for Glyn's leg it's a very slow way - but there are pleasures other than the pleasure of sheer speed, such as these little rocky bits, and the sudden steepening of the path as it turns into a new hollow of the valley. Also, there are no tussocks.

On the road through Abergwesyn my blisters started to boil out from under the bandage. Up a long grassy pass it was all getting a bit grim. Glyn lectured me about counting the blessings of my lithe young body and extracting pleasure despite the pain. Certainly his sufferings were greater than mine, but if I had his legs I wouldn't be going anywhere on them. I discovered that by running hard I could divert the pain of my feet to somewhere other than the brain. Doing the final two miles in fifteen minutes let me arrive feeling like a dispirited runner rather than a dispirited hobbler, and also in good condition for the Dragon shower! You fill the dangling black bucket with water from the boiler, haul it up the tent pole and open the sprinkler in its bottom. No wonder we won the War.

Chris was before me in the line for the medical sergeant: "Your Dad made me suffer in his time. Now I get my own back." He methodically goes over all the bits that hurt in Chris' ankle and prescribes: "rest it." That's a joke. Glyn was thrilled with the job done on his bad thigh - if only he didn't have the two bad ankles. I got 0.5cc of fluid drawn from my blister.

The sandstone cliffs of Carmarthen Fan

Quite a small one by Falklands War standards. "Planning to run on this tomorrow?" I wasn't sure. He injected TINCT BENZ, which made me go ooh aah for a while. After this ordeal, I'd have to run tomorrow – or rather, walk. It wouldn't be fun but I'd try not to groan too much. Bed, though, was deeply enjoyable for the few seconds it took to fall asleep.

Day 5: The Black Mountain

The final day to Carreg Cennen Castle started with a long, long road walk: thirteen miles of it, occasionally breaking into a shamble. Five minutes after the start Martin Stone and Helene Diamantides ran past with greetings – such a handsome couple. They had led the race for the first three days, but the flat fourth day had allowed Belton and McDermott to seize the lead by just four minutes.

At the back we formed, along with Chris and Dave, the walking wounded. Dave's friend fancied a go at the Bob Graham Round: would we send our schedule? What do we talk about during events? Other events.

The lanes eventually led to the impressive scarp of' Carmarthen Fan: old red sandstone and fresh grass. The grass and sandstone themselves had been denied us because the race might damage the path, but what had to be a red kite was soaring above the place, and the grass and sandstone looked good even from underneath. Below the red-and-green lay a lovely lake with an orange tent. Here we stopped to think.

Chris and Dave (both of course injured in their legs, though neither so badly as Glyn) planned to omit the descent to Glyntawe and two of the heavy limestone hills behind the scarp. We too should take this shortcut if we were to get through the tough ground in daylight. But how do you persuade Glyn, and for that matter Stefan, almost as stubborn and determined? The thinking was made more difficult by the TV camera that loomed close over the debate and my pig-dog German. (Fortunately, though, the programme was not scheduled for transmission to Pig-dog Germany, so that this searing bit of human interest didn't get used.)

"Wir mussen uber dieses sheissliches grund passen befor es nacht wird." The Paras catch 'sheissliche' and nod agreement. Glyn is not influenced by decaying shoes, decaying feet: still less by sheisslichkeit of ground, which is a plus. However, he was persuaded by other considerations. Young Stefan now had a twisted ankle of his own; and the descent to Glyntawe is an inelegant dogleg, spoiling the route, whereas Carmarthen Fan, the fine sandstone slice we just walked round the bottom of, could almost be justified as a rational straight line across the dogleg. Stefan seemed puzzled at being consulted over the route. It would only waste more time to enquire whether he understood what he'd agreed to.

Next we were to rise above the little lake on a near-vertical grass slope with a slanting path. Camera off, the man from Channel Four now existed and might be spoken to. He told stirring tales of the front runners, many hours ahead of us. Stone and Diamantides, a full seven minutes astray after yesterday's roads and tracks, took this slope direct, seizing back the lead in a short 750ft ascent. Great TV! "Not by chance," I told him. "All fixed up by Diamantides and Ian Waddell behind the food tent on Wednesday evening." He took a while to see the funny side of this joke.

I took the Diamantides/Stone line up the steep face, and enjoyed some hill-running over a couple of extra tops along the ridge. It's a splendid place with its steep grass sides and wide views: best hill since Cadair Idris. We pointed over the edge, explained to Stefan the joys of running down 2000ft of steep grass. He'll stick to the Hundred Kilometre.

He now realised that we'd cut out five miles of the race. He was upset, but it was the only way we'd finish at all. He even managed a brave joke: we should raise his waterproof as an orange tent on Carmarthen Fan and impose time penalty on everybody else for not visiting it.

The actual orange tent was in a small green swamp two miles away. The Lieutenant offered hot sweet tea and called us "bloody heroes". Wrong: it was just our way of having fun. Fun we must have been having, for here came another joke, for Ian Waddell this time: a man from the Council was after him. His notice, 'Dragon Race: please close the gate' should have been in Welsh.

We hobbled onwards into the limestone. It was nasty in bits: limestone boulder-fields are soapy-slippery but interesting, with sink-holes in the grass where underground caverns have collapsed. At the final orange tent we had a choice. There was the proper route over two small hills or, it now being 6.00pm, there was no shame in dropping round by the lanes. Of course, we were going over the two small hills.

We set off for the first of them. We now discovered that when Glyn had kindly given Chris some of his painkillers, he had actually given not some but all. At this moment along the little road behind us drove Chris Senior, getting into position for his final delivery of bananas. Forgetting the unhappy result of my previous attempt at being helpful, I flagged him down. No problem. Glyn could have one of Chris' painkillers.

It's an impressive large orange bomb, something-gesic. Ten minutes later, up on the hill, Glyn starts waving his arms around and shouting. Then he starts staggering – not that we weren't all doing that anyway. Forward progress becomes slow indeed as the light fades. It's a bit unsettling. Every few steps we take towards Tair Carn Uchaf, the going becomes harder. First it's heather, then it's deep heather, then it's deep heather with rocks underneath. Perhaps, as in the Paradox of the Arrow, we shall forever approach but never arrive.

Down at the castle they were filming runners as they climbed up out of the sunset – a special kink had been put into the route so that we should arrive out of the West. Meanwhile, we defied five separate leg injuries and the Greek philosopher Zeno by reaching the cairn of Tair Carn Uchaf.

"Glyn," I said, "let's get off this hill." "Nonshensh. Not even dark yet. Where's that other one they're sending us over?" "Glyn, your speech is slurred and you're in a bad way." "My shpeesh ish not shlurrrd!"

I tried to persuade Stefan, but Stefan was just as insistent on the last pile of boulders. "I didn't understand any of that," said Glyn cheerily. "You must have been speaking German." So – short of putting Glyn into his sleeping bag and tying the neck up very tight, which I wouldn't be able to do until he actually passed out – the decision was made. In fact there's a useful little path through the final boulders, while the descent afterwards, in full darkness, it is on heather so deep and soft that all it took to get down was leaning forward and flailing about a bit. My torch was weak: writing up my journal in the tent after lights-out had depleted the batteries. Glyn's torch was broken, but good Stefan's had a large and powerful beam. Down in the valley, Glyn gradually became coherent. Had I been over-reacting? Glyn always walks in a funny way.

We steered the two miles of path by torchlight and compass, searching each field-end for stile or waymark. "Are you sure this is the right track?" Glyn asked suddenly. I shone the torch onto the compass. South-east, and ten seconds ago it was North! Now compasses never break down, so it must be my brain not working any more: in which case we'd be wandering in circles here till our legs folded under us.

But no: it was in fact the compass. I was standing on an iron cattle grid completely covered over with mud. Glyn had his revenge for my disparagement of his mental state. Only Celtic intuition combined with the lingering remnants of the Something-gesic could have let him guess, though, the precise moment when I'd be standing over the buried metal...

The path changed direction nine times but Glyn's intuition, my compass and Stefan's torch got us through. It took a long time but it was fun. And so, at 9:00pm, we reached the castle. We'd finished. We weren't even last!

They offered free beer. But there are no riotous scenes in the food tent. Most people are enjoying simpler pleasures like

Winners Martin Stone and Helene Diamantides at the finishing line at Carreg Cennen Castle   Photo: Nicola Gillham

dry footwear, sleep, and not having to get up at five in the morning and start running. Stone and Diamantides lost their way and their lead in the limestone, but eventually won the race. Their big advantage was being slightly less injured in their legs than the pursuing pair.

After all the time penalties have been worked out, we were 13th out of 17 pairs. But since 27 pairs started the race, we're actually in the first half of the field! We achieved our final climb, to the tall limestone castle set on its tall limestone rock, and got a brass dragon paperweight engraved 'survivor'. The Swede took notes on Glyn for his running magazine: "He has been in the pants for how long you say? Fourteen years?" We sat around appreciating our paperweights and telling one another about our injuries.

Not Glyn, though. He didn't approve of the tall limestone castle, and limped away under his rucksack to finish this thing properly. He was walking the final 30 mls to the Gower Coast.

Doing Lots of Tops
by Ronald Turnbull

The Welsh 3000s: How to Run Them
Walking the Welsh 3000s
Running the Paddy Buckley Round

The Welsh 3000s: How to Run Them

If you're an athlete with serious intentions on Donnelly's record, all of what I write below will be useful to you except that you'll already know it. You should join the Eryri club, where you'll find the detailed advice, support and encouragement to clip those crucial minutes and seconds off the fifteen peaks. Donnelly himself is a member.

Lesser athletes will want to undertake the run just because it's such a good one. For them, the first runner's record, that of Thomas Firbank, might be a more realistic target. His time of 8 hrs 25 min (his wife Esme achieved 9 hrs 29 on the same day) should be achievable, but not easily achievable. In its day it was a famous, even outrageous, run; and the account in *I Bought a Mountain* will have your PB trainers twitching out from under the cupboard.

If that's too slow for you, you could set your sights on Joss Naylor's time of 4 hrs 46. After all, even some of your friends who aren't runners have heard of Joss Naylor.

Direction: Snowdon is 469 ft higher than Foel-fras, so that the northbound direction is downhill. Against that we must set the fact that unpleasantly steep slopes cause less time disadvantage when taken in ascent. On the Welsh 3000s southbound, the main nasty downslope is off Pen yr Ole Wen; the one off Elidir Fawr is steep but grassy. Northbound, you have tricky rock-work off Crib Goch; the Llyn Glas variant reduces the steep stuff to 1000 ft, which is why it's quicker. You also have Tryfan.

Record attempts have always started on Snowdon. By my reckoning, the extra 500ft southbound costs 7.5 minutes: the extra 150m of nasty descent saves 3 minutes. If you're strong uphill but bad at coming down Tryfan, you might consider the backwards approach. Northbound has been the "official" direction; break the record backwards and cause some serious head scratching in the inner councils of the Fell Running Association.

For the runner or strong walker who just wants a superb day out, the southbound traverse has advantages. The grassy slopes of Foel-fras offer bivvy sites far superior to the porch of the Snowdon 'Hotel'. The scrambles of Tryfan's North Ridge and Bristly Ridge can be taken in ascent: the intrepid could even take in the Jammed Boulder Gully of Crib Goch. The Pinnacle Ridge of Crib y Ddysgl makes a splendid climax... and a schedule timed to arrive 10 mins before the last train down Snowdon will add momentum to the entire trip.

Food: If you're unable to drink because of no appetite and no saliva, you're dehydrated. If you're unable to eat because of feeling sick, then you've been going too fast; the digestive system needs energy and your legs have used it all up. In either case the remedy is to slow down, and take a glucose drink (such as Staminade) in plenty of water. The ability to eat should return within half an hour.

If you're actually being sick, you've let things go too far. Stop, take the glucose, and spend ten minutes in some useful stationary activity such as taking photos or repairing your feet. A little more glucose, a mouthful of rice pudding, and continue slowly. With luck, new man (or woman) will kick in within half an hour.

The ideal menu is carbohydrate: slow-burning starch, plus a bit of instant-energy sugar. Popular foodstuffs are honey sandwiches, flapjack, rock buns, bananas, Mr Kipling's Bramley apple pies, custard, rice pudding, biscuits, muesli bars... perhaps not all at once.

A recent development is the powdered form of complex carbohydrate (starch) food such as Maxim, H5 or Isostar. These can be mixed with water and carried in a specially designed fuel tank between the shoulder blades. A plastic tube lets you sip at the stuff continually - maybe this makes you feel like an astronaut, maybe it makes you feel like a patient in intensive care. Either way, a happy stomach means happy legs and more than repays the extra weight. (The same firms do glucose drinks, too, so you have to read the packets to work out which is which. Or you can mix them to create a powdered honey sandwich.)

Drink: Roy has carefully detailed the water sources; use them, every one. If it's hot, carry a small waterbottle in the bumbag.

Starting too fast: ensures that you stop having fun and start suffering rather early on in the run, and also end up finishing rather slowly. There are three ways to avoid:

Self-knowledge: if you can't chat to your companions, you're going too fast. If you can't eat in comfort, you're going too fast

Schedule: the schedules in Section 8 are to help you go slow enough. If you're going even slower than the schedule, then stick the thing in your pocket and forget it. You're allowed to go faster than the schedule on the two descent sections; at the road breaks; and over the Carneddau. But elsewhere, stick to it.

Heart rate monitor: When you got the monitor, there was a piece of paper in the bottom of the box that blew away and got lost. This explained how to calculate your Aerobic Threshold, which is the heart rate at which you're using up oxygen faster than you can breathe. You want to get your heart rate to 80% of this level and keep it there. (On downhills and scrambling sections you won't be able to, though.)

Fitness: ordinary training should be supplemented by endurance outings: trips over the hills of at least three hours. On the actual crossing you won't run uphill; it's quicker overall not to. But in training, run uphill. It hurts so much, it just has to be good for you.

Injury: Sprained ankles, and injuries to the ligaments and tendons of the leg, can be rendered bearable to run on with Ibuprofen or Aspirin. Stronger painkillers such as codeine are banned by the British Athletics Federation, to which the Fell Running Association is affiliated. They also affect the judgement, causing you to run over cliffs, into wrong valleys, snowstorms etc. Sprained ankles can be helped by dipping them in cold water for ten minutes. These measures treat the symptoms: running on when injured makes the injury worse and the sensible thing is to stop. But then, few really sensible people run hills.

Safety: The gear carried by the normal hillrunner (lightweight waterproofs, hat, gloves, thermal long johns and top) means that if the weather turns nasty, you only keep warm by keeping moving. If the weather turns nasty and then you injure yourself or get exhausted, then the Mountain Rescue will eventually find you, but the anorexic chap with the scythe will probably get there first. So you either

* Carry more gear (e.g. proper survival bag) OR
* Face death

Most hillrunners seem to go for the second option.

What you carry will depend on the weather, the weather forecast, how fat you are (skinny people get hypothermic sooner), whether you're running solo, and your personal risk/speed trade-off. The minimum that must be carried on long fell races in Britain is

Waterproof trousers and top
2 oz high-calorie food
map & compass
whistle

Even with a support runner alongside, I'd carry that much. Support runners often drop behind and get abandoned.

Hypothermia and Heat-stroke

Which you get depends on the weather. Hypothermia is made more likely by not eating enough, while heat-stroke is seriously bad dehydration. Both conditions kill, and kill quite suddenly.

In either case the early symptom is tiredness - but you'll be feeling tired anyway, so may not notice. Later symptoms are irrationality, staggering gait, slurred speech and loss of judgement. "There's nothing wrong with my shpeesh," you'll say, while running round in circles in that snowstorm. Unconsciousness calls for urgent action by your support runner – awkward if you haven't got a support runner.

Supported or Solo?

Failing reincarnation, solo lightweight hillrunning is as close as you'll ever get to being a bird. To stretch your legs across the smooth Carneddau at dawn when everyone else is asleep; to whizz down off Y Garn with wind in your hair and dip your sweaty head in the Llyn y Cwn; to drop like a loose boulder into Cwm Glas with a single boggy footfall every three yards; all this is very good. It is also rather risky. You're relying on your speed to keep you warm, your strong legs to get you off the hill.

If you know what you're doing, then do it. If you're not sure – perhaps you're a roadrunner who got fed up with running on roads, rather than a hillwalker who's speeded up – then find a support runner. Support runners are fun too, and warm friendships have been formed along these chilly ridges.

Walking the Welsh 3000s

The technical advice for runners on the 3000s can also be consulted by walkers. Walkers just have to take all of my suggestions there a bit less seriously. For most walkers the aim will be to complete the walk within the day. The secondary aim will be to enjoy doing so, apart from the scree-climb to Glyder Fawr, it would be futile to attempt to enjoy that.

For those who seek to walk the fifteen peaks, four commandments are carved deep into the rocks of Snowdon.

> Start early
> Start slowly
> Eat lots
> Drink lots

For those who break even one of these commandments, special pains and torments await in the place appointed for such punishment: that place being roughly 1000 ft above Ogwen Cottage on the slopes of Pen yr Ole Wen.

Start early: Bivvy on Snowdon and you're bound to start early, you'll be too cold to lie around. But even if you sleep at sea-level, get onto the Pig Track before dawn. You'll find that uphill in the dark at daybreak is a very different game from downhill in the dark when you got benighted. Uphill in the dark's easier than downhill in the dark; your toes are unblistered; and you knew you were going to do it so you put fresh batteries in the torch. A quite unnecessary reward for such sensible behaviour comes with the looking down on the sleeping streetlights of

Anglesey, the gleam of Llyn Llydaw under the moon, the final blaze of sunrise across Colwyn Bay.

Start slowly: Start slower than your usual speed. You're going to be tired at the end. Why start getting tired at the beginning?

Eat lots: To go twice as far as usual you need at least twice as much food. Take three lunches. Don't wait till you stop to eat. Fill your pockets with muesli bars and practice in-flight refuelling.

Drink lots: Don't wait till you're thirsty – you're dehydrated long before that. Early dehydration and hunger are both mistaken by the ignorant brain for tiredness. Know better than your brain: eat, drink, and keep going.

Fitness: the most enjoyable way to get fit for hillwalking is to walk over hills. The time to do the Welsh 3000s is a fortnight after the end of ten days of intensive training in Scotland or Lake District. If you want to train specially for your long walk, then exercise for 30 minutes, three times a week, for a month. The exercise should be vigorous enough to make you pant and sweat a bit. Strolling to work isn't enough unless you spend all day strolling to work. Jogging, cycling or swimming are convenient and effective.

Safety: very tired walkers have trouble thinking straight. The Welsh 3000s are an unaccompanied walk only for those experienced walkers whose hillcraft is almost instinctive. Such will make their own decisions on what to leave behind in order to lighten the sack. I would carry:

> a long-sleeved and a long-legged garment, as well as
> lightweight waterproof top and bottom, hat & gloves
> survival bag
> map compass & whistle and torch
> food (1 kg: sandwiches, Mars/snickers, muesli bars)
> small water-bottle, for the Carneddau

Some sensible person should know what you're doing. Give them a specific time to call out the mountain rescue if they haven't heard from you. If you carry that survival bag, this specific time can reasonably be dawn the day after.

Running Paddy Buckley

The advice about starting slowly, eating lots, using the schedule and so on – all this applies to any attempt on the Paddy

Buckley 24-hour circuit, but more so. Start even more slowly, eat even more, etc.

The Buckley Round is that little bit more than the ordinary fit hillrunner can realistically hope to achieve in 24 hrs. Paddy Buckley himself never quite managed it, and neither did I. Only make a serious attempt if you're more than averagely talented, very fit indeed, and totally familiar with the route. You'll probably already have done the Lake District's Bob Graham Round in around 22 hrs; this is a useful training run for the Buckley one.

If you are such a one as I describe, then I can only gaze in awe at your mighty calf-muscles, your far-away obsessive eyes, and marvel at the easy competence with which you handle the Camelbak food system and the electronic heart monitor.

About the Route
Three types of person attempt the Buckley Round. There are those who prepare by walking, or running, every step of the route beforehand, in thick mist if they can get it, making careful notes on fence junctions and the shapes of summit cairns. Others rely on map skills sharpened to perfection by the simple process of getting lost on Mountain Marathons. A third group just start running and hope for the best - a forlorn hope in a world where tops and even bottoms suddenly go away into clouds, fences sink into the bog and get rebuilt somewhere slightly different and even the OS 'Outdoor Leisure' map has mistakes on.

None of the three will benefit from a detailed step-by-step route guide given in the 4-day backpack: the first two don't need it, and the third doesn't have time to read it, having lost half an hour already on the wrong summit of Moelwyn Bach.

This is not work for words. For this you use your map.

When your tent leaks in the middle of the night, you hunt out your moleskin plasters and see what you can do to patch over the holes. In the same spirit, the words below attempt to patch over a few small holes in the map.

1: Elidir Fach: Two bridges cross the Afon Rhythallt between the two lakes. The western one is a footbridge, served by a rough path. The eastern one, beside Llyn Peris, is the bridge crossed by the motor road. (The OS Outdoor Leisure map has these the wrong way round.) From the road bridge the path suggested in 'Buckley: the Backpack' zigzags up between slates to the horizontal track at 200m altitude marked as public footpath. In the past, Buckley contenders have continued from here up the inclines. This is now blocked by fences and notices 'keep to public footpath'. For runners the quickest alternative is to head out of Llanberis SE on the A4086 for 1½ miles to take the right of way from the head of Llyn Peris. This is nastier, but quicker than the alternative route for walkers in Section 5.

Ogwen: For descent of Tryfan see Welsh 3000s Section 1. This is quicker than the descent described in the 4-day Backpack.

29: Cnicht: The right-of-way leading to the foot of the small reservoir 654466 has no existence on the ground that I could detect. Nevertheless this is a satisfactory way to Cnicht, the intimidating SE slope of which yields at this point, if trudged up with sufficient persistence.

30: Bryn Banog: The right-of-way from Aberglaslyn is lost under deep bracken. Send wide friends in advance to trample the way. If you have friends who happen to be cattle, they'll do a fine job for you.

34: Y Gyrn: After this summit, descend left (NW) to stone wall, and follow this right to traverse into Bwlch-y-Ddwy-elor. *Rhyd Ddu:* The footpath running eastwards across the valley floor to the car park is worth seeking out.

Section 8

Schedules & Data

WELSH 3000s

		SCHEDULE J			SCHEDULE F		
		mls	ft	min	ETA	min	ETA
1	Snowdon				0:00		0:00
2	Carnedd Ugain	.5	200	5	0:05	9	0:09
3	Crib Goch	.9	200	19	0:24	32	0:41
	A 4086 Blaen-y-nant	1.6		21	0:45	36	1:17
	Nant Peris	1.3		7	0:52	11	1:28
Section		**4.3**	**400**	**52 min**	**1 hr 28**		
	rest					10	1:38
4	Elidir Fawr	2.3	2700	43	1:35	72	2:50
5	Y Garn	2.2	800	24	1:59	39	3:29
6	Glyder Fawr	1.4	1000	20	2:19	33	4:02
7	Glyder Fach	.9	300	9	2:28	16	4:18
8	Tryfan	1.0	600	18	2:46	31	4:49
	Ogwen	1.2		19	3:05	32	5:21
Section		**9.0**	**5400**	**2 hr 13**	**3 hr 43**		
rest						10	5:31
9	Pen yr Ole Wen	1.1	2300	33	3:38	57	6:28
10	Carnedd Dafydd	1.0	400	11	3:49	20	6:48
11	Yr Elen	2.4	300	20	4:09	34	7:22
12	Carnedd Llewelyn	.9	600	13	4:22	22	7:44
13	Foel Grach	1.1	100	9	4:31	15	7:59
14	Garnedd Uchaf	.7	100	6	4:37	10	8:09
15	Foel-fras	1.0	200	9	4:46	16	8:25
Section		**8.2**	**4000**	**1 hr 41**	**2 hr 54**		
Welsh 3000s		**21.5**	**9800**	**4 hr 46**	**8 hrs 25**		

Schedule J is calculated to equal the time of Joss Naylor, and Schedule F, of Thomas Firbank.

See also actual times of Colin Donnelly and Angela Carson on pages 17 and 18.

Notes

Calculated schedules take account of distance and ascent, but also of rough ground and nasty descents. A slowing-down factor of 6% is included after Ogwen. Donnelly slowed down by 20%, confirming his suggestion of a poor finish over the Carneddau.

Distances are measured off map. For convenience of calculation they make no allowance for wiggles, distance up slope. For boasting purposes, 10% may be added.

Descents to Blaen-y-nant, Ogwen: descent-times vary widely with the skill of the descender. Donnelly, a demon descender, improved on calculated times by 25%.

For walkers, comparitive times for the sections will be:

up Snowdon	2 hrs
Snowdon massif	2 hrs
Glyders	6 hrs
Caneddau	5 hrs
Total Welsh 3000s	14hrs
off Foel-fras	*1hr*

For North to South walkers:

up Foel-fras	2 hrs
Carneddau	4 hrs
Glyders	6 hrs
Snowdon massif	3hrs
Total Welsh 3000s	14hrs
off Snowdon	*1 hr*

The Paddy Buckley Round

Paddy Buckley's 24-hour Round may be run in either direction, and started at any point, and at any time of day or night. The choice of direction is determined by the amount of steep or difficult downhill. The anticlockwise direction would involve such descents off Pen yr Ole Wen, Tryfan, Glyder Fawr, Elidir Fawr, Cribau Tregalan, Moel Hebog, Cnicht and Craigysgafn. This direction is rarely attempted.

Given the clockwise direction, steep downhill again determines the choice of start-point. As you go round you go slower, but the effect of tiredness is most marked on tough descents. (Tryfan tired takes 50 minutes instead of 30.) Clockwise, the tough descent is Tryfan, with lesser bad bits off Glyder Fach, Yr Aran (Snowdon), and Pen Llithrig y Wrach. Thus a start at Rhyd-Ddu or Llanberis is suggested.

Darkness has little effect on road or uphill progress, considerable effect on horizontal boulderfields and most effect on those difficult descents. Tricky route finding over the rocks and bogs of the Siabod/Moelwyn group also asks for daylight.

I prefer to have the night section early in the run. With the uncertainties of night still ahead, it's tempting to run faster than the schedule: and running too fast at the start is the commonest bad mistake.

Paddy Buckley Round Schedule

The following schedule is for Llanberis start at 1:00 am and clockwise circuit.

		mls	ft	CALC	min	ETA	
1: Glyders							
Llanberis						0100	
1	Elidir Fach	1.8	2300	63	53	0153	
2	Elidir Fawr	.5	500	15	17	0210	
3	Mynydd Perfedd	.9	200	14	14	0224	
4	Foel-goch	.5	400	13	12	0236	
5	Y Garn	1.2	600	25	22	0258	
6	Glyder Fawr	1.4	1000	35	35	0333	daylight
7	Glyder Fach	.9	300	16	16	0349	
8	Tryfan	.9	600	22	35	0424	
	Ogwen	1.2		15	30	0454	
	Total	**9.3**	**5900**	**3:45**	**3:54**		
rest					10		
2: Carneddau							
Ogwen dep						0504	
9	Pen yr Ole Wen	1.1	2300	55	56	0600	
10	Carnedd Dafydd	.9	400	18	16	0616	
11	Carnedd Llewelyn	1.9	400	30	30	0646	
12	Pen yr Helgi Du	1.3	400	23	26	0712	
13	Pen Llithrig y Wrach	1.2	600	25	23	0735	
Plas y Brenin		3.1		37	37	0812	
	Total	**9.5**	**4100**	**3:08**	**3:08**		
rest					10		
3: Northern Moelwyns							
Plas y Brenin dep						0822	
14	Moel Siabod	2.2	2300	68	58	0920	
15	Clogwyn Bwlch-y-maen	1.7	100	22	18	0938	
16	Carnedd y Gribau	.5	200	10	10	0948	
17	Cerrig Cochion	1.9	600	34	38	1026	
18	Moel Meirch	.5	400	13	14	1040	
19	Ysgafel Wen	1.0	300	17	22	1102	
20	Mynydd Llynnau'r Cwn	.2	100	4	4	1106	
21	Unnamed (672m)	.4	100	7	7	1113	
22	Moel Druman	.5	200	10	10	1123	
23	Allt-fawr	.6	300	13	14	1137	
Bwlch Cwmorthin		1.1		13	18	1155	
	Total	**10.6**	**4600**	**3:39**	**3:33**		
rest					10		

Paddy Buckley Round Continued

		mls	ft	CALC	min	ETA	
4: Moelwyns & Cnicht							
Bwlch Cwmorthin dep						1205	
24	Foel Ddu	.4	500	15	15	1220	
25	Moel-yr-hydd	.3	300	10	9	1229	
26	Moelwyn Bach	1.5	700	33	31	1300	
27	Craigysgafn	.5	300	12	13	1313	
28	Moelwyn Mawr	.4	300	11	10	1323	
Bwlch Cwmorthin (near)		1.1		14	14	1337	
29	Cnicht	1.4	1000	38	38	1415	
Aberglaslyn		3.7	200	52	50	1505	
	Total	**9.3**	**3300**	**3:05**	**3:00**		
rest					15		
5: Eifionydd							
Aberglaslyn dep						1520	
30	Bryn Banog	1.7	1700	55	50	1610	
31	Moel Hebog	1.1	1100	36	34	1644	
32	Moel yr Ogof	.9	400	20	20	1704	
33	Moel Lefn	.4	200	9	12	1716	
34	Y Gyrn	1.1	400	22	24	1740	
35	Mynydd-y-ddwy-elor	.4	200	9	12	1752	
36	Trum y Ddysgl	.9	800	27	27	1819	
37	Mynydd Drws-y-coed	.4	200	9	9	1828	
38	Y Garn	.5	100	8	12	1840	
Rhyd Ddu		1.4		18	26	1906	
	Total	**8.8**	**5100**	**3:33**	**3:46**		
rest					15		
6: Snowdon							
Rhyd Ddu dep						1921	
39	Craig Wen	2.5	1400	64	57	2018	
40	Yr Aran	.6	600	21	19	2037	
41	Cribau Tregalan	1.4	1400	49	55	2134	
42	Yr Wyddfa (Snowdon)	.6	600	21	18	2152	
43	Carnedd Ugain	.5	200	11	11	2203	nightfall
44	Moel Cynghorion	2.0	600	41	49	2252	
45	Foel Goch	1.2	500	27	23	2315	
46	Foel Gron	.5	400	15	16	2331	
47	Moel Eilio	.9	400	21	16	2347	
Llanberis		2.9		41	35	0022	
Total		**13.1**	**6100**	**5:11**	**5:01**		

Paddy Buckley Round Continued

		mls	ft	calc. time	sched
1	Glyders	9.3	5900	3:38	3:54
2	Carneddau	9.5	4100	3:08	3:08
3	Northern Moelwyn	10.6	4600	3:39	3:33
4	Moelwyn & Cnicht	9.3	3300	3:05	3:00
5	Eifionydd	8.8	5100	3:33	3:46
6	Snowdon	13.1	6100	5:11	5:01
	rest			1:00	1:00
	Total	61	29000	23:14	23:22

Calculated timings are derived from Naismith formula (1000 ft up = 1 mile extra) and a 12 mins/mile speed: Glyders, Carneddau, Moelywns to (15) Clogwyn Bwlch-y-maen; 13 min/mile: Remaining Moelwyns, Eifionydd and 14 min/mile: Snowdon Range. The scheduled time takes into account the rough nature of the terrain and previous recorded times.

These tops are not marked on Landranger or Outdoor Leisure maps:

19	Ysgafel Wen	664488	
20	Mynydd Llynau'r Cwn	664485	669m
22	Unnamed summit	667481	672m
28	Craigysgafn	660445	
30	Bryn Banog	576457	529m
34	Y Gyrn	553501	
35	Mynydd-y-Ddwy-elor	549504	466m
41	Cribau Tregalan	605536	

Daylight Hours

The table lists times of sunset and sunrise for Snowdonia. Dawn and dusk are, roughly, when it's possible to read a map by natural light. Useful light to walk or run by extends up to half an hour longer if skies are clear. All times are British Summer Time except March.

	Dawn	Sunrise	Sunset	Dusk
June 21	4:10	4:55	21:45	22:30
May 21, July 21	4:30	5:15	21:20	22:05
April 21, Aug 21	5:30	6:10	20:30	21:05
September 21 (BST)	6:45	7:15	19:15	19:50
March 21 (GMT)	5:45	6:15	18:15	18:50

Overnight runners on the Buckley round will want to know about the moon as well as the sun. Dates of the full moon can be found in diaries and on calendars. On the days around the full moon, there will be useful light for the greater part of the night. Even with slight cloud cover, this light of the full moon can be enough to see your way by. (You still need the torch, though, to read the map with.)

During the week before the full moon, there is moonlight during the first part of the night only. During the week after full moon, moonlight is in the hours before dawn. During the week either side of the new moon, there is little useful moonlight.

Precise times of moonrise and moonset are in Whitaker's Almanack. Even small public libraries should have a copy.

Other Data

Maps
For the Welsh 3000s, the Welsh 1000s and the Snowdon Horseshoe you can get by with the Landranger 1:50000 No 115 "Snowdon & Surrounding Area" but the latest double sided Outdoor Leisure 1:25000 No.17 "Snowdonia: Snowdon & the Conwy Valley Areas" is far superior for route finding as it shows fences, walls and details many more of the crags. RT says it's a bit bulky and hard to use for runners though.

The excellent Harveys 'Snowdonia West' and 'Snowdonia North' cover the route. They're waterproof and will not disintegrate in the rain or snow, which is useful – but you'll have to carry two maps. OS Pathfinders SH65/75 plus SH66/76 (1:25000) cover the 3000s route but not the return to Aber.

On the Paddy Buckley Round you'll need in addition the Outdoor Leisure Map, "Harlech & Bala' or the Landranger 124 'Dolgellau' or Harveys 'Snowdonia West'.

For the Dragon's Back you'll need OS Landranger Nos 115, 124, 135, 147 and 160.

Transport

By Railway
1   North Wales Coastal line via Llandudno calls at Bangor. Link from Llandudno Junction to Conwy Valley Stations of Tal-y-cafn, Llanrwst and Betws-y-Coed.
2 Porthmadog via rail from Shrewsbury via Machynlleth

By bus
Local Bus timetables including the very useful Snowdon Sherpas Service can be obtained from:-
National Park Office, Penrhyndeudraeth,Gwynedd LL48 6LS. Tel:01766 770274 or County Planning Officer,Gwynedd County Council,County Offices, Caernarfon, Gwynedd LL55 1SH. Tel: 01286 672255
Please enclose a 9" x 6" s.a.e.

Accommodation and Eating Out

Youth Hostels
Pen-y-Pass, Nantgwynant,Caernarfon,Gwynedd LL55 4NY.
Tel. 01286 870428   GR 647557
Llanberis, Llwyn Celyn,Llanberis,Gwynedd LL55 4SR
Tel. 01286 870280   GR 574596
Snowdon Ranger,   Rhyd Ddu,   Caernarfon,   Gwynedd LL54
Tel 01286 650391   GR 565550
Bryn Gwynant, Nantgwynant,Caernarfon,Gwynedd LL55 4NP
Tel. 0176686 251   GR 640513
Idwal Cottage, Nr Bethesda, Bangor,Gwynedd LL57 3LZ
Tel. 01248 600225   GR 648604
Rowen, Rhiw Farm, Rowen, Nr Conwy.
Tel. 01492 530627 or 01222 231370   GR 747721
Closed in Winter & limited opening in the summer months.
Conwy, Larkhill, Sychnant Pass Rd, Conwy, Gwynedd LL32 8AJ
Tel. 01492 593571   GR 775773
Enquiries to Wales Regional Office Tel 01222 231370 or 01492 530627
Youth Hostel Association National Office: Trevelyan House, 8 St
Stephen's Hill, St. Albans, Herts AL1 2DY

Hotels
Many at Capel Curig, Betws y Coed, Beddgelert, Bangor and Caernarfon.
Up to date details can be obtained from the Tourist Information Centre,
Oriel Pendeitsh, Caernarfon, Gwynedd LL55 2PB. Tel 01286 672232.

Campsites
Nant Peris GR 604587 (not marked on current map)
LLanberis GR 563633
Beddgelert GR 577491
Betws y Garmon GR 536575 & 546567
Gwern Gof Isaf GR 686601
Capel Curig GR 743572
Dwygyfylchi GR 730770

Cafes
Pete's Eats, Llanberis - has been described as the best café in the world
Pinnacle Café, Capel Curig.
Gorphwysfa Café, Pen y Pass
Snowdon View Café, Capel Curig

Good Pubs
Cobdens, Capel Curig - climbers' bar built into a rockface at the rear of
the building. Bar meals and accommodation available
Bryn Twrch, Capel Curig - pleasant accommodation available.
Ty'n y Coed, Capel Curig – bustling pub. Bar meals and accommodation
Vaynol Arms, Nant Peris – Bar meals, accommodation available

Good Pubs (continued)

Royal Victoria, Llanberis – Bar meals, accommodation
Padarn Lake Hotel, Llanberis – Bar meals, accommodation
Royal Oak Hotel, Betws-y-Coed – bar meals and accommodation
Pen-y-Gwryd Hotel, Nantgwynant– good atmosphere. Accommodation available.
Cwellyn Arms, Rhyd Ddu, Good bar meals
The Heights Hotel, Llanberis, for BMC Members. Has a climbing wall in the back bar. B & B and bunkhouse type accommodation.

Some Useful Addresses

Fell Runners Association
  Peter Bland, 34a Kirkland, Kendal, Cumbria LA9 5AD

Long Distance Walkers' Association. Membership Secretary
  Geoff Saunders, 117 Higher Lane, Rainford, St Helens,
  Merseyside WA11 8BQ

The Ramblers Association:
1-5 Wandsworth Rd, London SW8 2XX

Wales Tourist Board
Brunel House, 2 Fitzalan Rd, Cardiff CF2 1UY

Backpackers Club, Jim and Maggie Beed, 49 Lyndhurst Rd, Exmouth
EX8 3DS

Useful Reading

The Welsh Peaks - Poucher (Constable)
Guide to Wales' 3000 Foot Mountains - H. Mulholland (Mulholland Wirral)
The Ridges of Snowdonia - Steve Ashton (Cicerone)
Snowdonia to the Gower - John Gillham (Baton Wicks/Diadem)
A Welsh Coast to Coast – John Gillham (Cicerone)
Hillwalking in Snowdonia- E.G. Rowland (Cicerone)
Hillwalking in Wales Vols 1 & 2 Peter Herman (Cicerone)
The Summits of Snowdonia - Terry Marsh (Hale)
On Foot in Snowdonia - Bob Allen (Michael Joseph)
I Bought a Mountain - Thomas Firbank (Harrap)
Wild Wales - George Borrow (Fontana)
The Mountains of England and Wales Vol 1 Wales - John and Anne
Nuttall (Cicerone)
Backpacking in Wales - Showell Styles (Hale)

Glossary of Welsh Words

Aber	river mouth	Ffridd	enclosed grazing land
Afon	river		
Arddu	black crag	Glas/las	blue, green
Bach/fach	small	Gwyn	white
Bedd	grave	Gwynt	wind
Betws	chapel	Hendre	winter dwelling
Blaen	head of valley		
Bont/pont	bridge	Isaf	lower
Bwlch	pass	LLan	church or blessed place
bws	bus		
Cae	field	Lllwybr Cyhoeddus	public footpath
Caer	fort		
Carnedd/Garnedd	cairn	Llwyd	grey
Capel	chapel	Llyn	lake
Carreg/garreg	stone	Maen	stone
Castell	castle	Maes	field/meadow
Cefn	ridge	Moch	pig
Cors/gors	bog	Moel/foel	featureless hill
Clogwyn	cliff		
Coch/goch	red	Mynydd	mountain
Coed	wood	Nant	stream
Craig	crag	Ogof	cave
Crib	sharp ridge	Pant	clearing, hollow
Cwm	coomb		
Cwn	dog	Pen	peak
Dinas	hill fort(or town)	Person	cascade
		Plas	mansion
Diolch	thank you	Pwll	pool
Du/ddu	black	Rhaeadr	waterfall
Drum/trum	ridge	Rhyd	ford
Drws	door	Saeth(au)	arrow(s)
Dyffryn	valley	Troed	foot of
Dwr	water	Twll	cavern
Eglwys	church	Ty	house
Esgair	ridge	Uchaf	high, higher
Eryri	eagles abode	Waun	moor
Fawr/mawr	large	Wen	white
Felin/melin	mill	Wrach	witch
Ffordd	road	Y, Yr	the
Ffynnon	spring	Ynys	Island

Other Titles From Grey Stone Books

The Famous Highland Drove Walk by Irvine Butterfield

Irvine Butterfield, the author of best selling book The High Mountains of Britain and Ireland, takes his readers in the hoofprints of the last drove in 1981, where 29 bullocks and a cow called Matililda recreated a historical journey across the Highlands of Scotland from the Isle of Skye to the mart at Crieff in Perthshire. He interweaves their story with background history and legend, and offers walkers alternative high and low routes enabling them to plan their own version of this romantic journey across seven great mountain ranges. Illustrated with both colour and black and white photos, maps and sketches.

Paperback   £9.95   ISBN 09515996-5-8

Across Scotland on Foot by Ronald Turnbull.

Highly acclaimed by the press, this 160-page book gives its readers six inspirational coast-to-coast routes across Scotland plus ideas and practical advice for planning their own. An ideal present for fell runners and walkers.

Paperback   £5.95   ISBN 09515996-4-x

Peaks of the Yorkshire Dales by John Gillham & Phil Iddon

A popular book that describes 31 mainly circular walks to the highest peaks in the Yorkshire Dales.The celebrated mountains of Ingleborough and Pen-y-Ghent are featured alongside lesser-known summits such as Great Coum above Dent and Rye Loaf Hill above Settle. There are 18 full-page colour photos and the maps are 3D panoramas.

Paperback   £8.95   ISBN 09515996-1-5

Bowland & The South Pennines by John Gillham

This is a celebration of some of England's wildest uplands – all within reach of the towns and cities of Lancashire, Yorkshire and Greater Manchester. John Gillham describes 33 walks - some to Bowland's - heather moors and some to the lofty gritstone-capped summits of the South Pennines. Phil Iddon describes routes to Pendle Hill, which lies sandwiched between the two ranges. There are 12 full-page colour photos and many black and white photos - the maps are 3D panoramas.

Hardback   £9.95   ISBN 09515996-0-7

The Bowland Dales Traverse by John Gillham

The Bowland-Dales Traverse is a long-distance route spanning 85 miles between Garstang near Preston to Richmond in Yorkshire, threading through some of the loveliest hill country of the Forest of Bowland and the Yorkshire Dales. The 64-page pocket book is illustrated by line drawings and black &white photos.

Paperback   £2.95   ISBN 09515996-2-3

All the books should be available at your local bookstore. In the case of any difficulty they can also be ordered post-free from **Cordee** 3a DeMontfort Street, Leicester LE1 7HD. Prices correct at time of printing (1997) and are based on the present zero rate of VAT .